THE PELICAN SHAKESPEARE
GENERAL EDITORS

STEPHEN ORGEL
A. R. BRAUNMULLER

The Life of King Henry the Fifth

The American comedian William Davidge
as Pistol, c. 1850

William Shakespeare

The Life of
King Henry the Fifth

EDITED BY CLAIRE MCEACHERN

PENGUIN BOOKS

PENGUIN BOOKS
Published by the Penguin Group
Penguin Putnam Inc., 375 Hudson Street,
New York, New York 10014, U.S.A.
Penguin Books Ltd, 27 Wrights Lane,
London W8 5TZ, England
Penguin Books Australia Ltd, Ringwood,
Victoria, Australia
Penguin Books Canada Ltd, 10 Alcorn Avenue,
Toronto, Ontario, Canada M4V 3B2
Penguin Books (N.Z.) Ltd, 182–190 Wairau Road,
Auckland 10, New Zealand

Penguin Books Ltd, Registered Offices:
Harmondsworth, Middlesex, England

The Life of King Henry the Fifth edited by Louis B. Wright and
Virginia Freund published in the United States of America
in Penguin Books 1957
The Life of King Henry the Fifth edited by Alfred Harbage
published 1966
Revised edition published 1972
This new edition edited by Claire McEachern published 1999

5 7 9 10 8 6 4

Copyright © Penguin Books Inc., 1957, 1966, 1972
Copyright © Penguin Putnam Inc., 1999
All rights reserved

ISBN 0-14-07.1458-8

Printed in the United States of America
Set in Garamond
Designed by Virginia Norey

Contents

Publisher's Note

IT IS ALMOST half a century since the first volumes of the Pelican Shakespeare appeared under the general editorship of Alfred Harbage. The fact that a new edition, rather than simply a revision, has been undertaken reflects the profound changes textual and critical studies of Shakespeare have undergone in the past twenty years. For the new Pelican series, the texts of the plays and poems have been thoroughly revised in accordance with recent scholarship, and in some cases have been entirely reedited. New introductions and notes have been provided in all the volumes. But the new Shakespeare is also designed as a successor to the original series; the previous editions have been taken into account, and the advice of the previous editors has been solicited where it was feasible to do so.

Certain textual features of the new Pelican Shakespeare should be particularly noted. All lines are numbered that contain a word, phrase, or allusion explained in the glossarial notes. In addition, for convenience, every tenth line is also numbered, in italics when no annotation is indicated. The intrusive and often inaccurate place headings inserted by early editors are omitted (as is becoming standard practice), but for the convenience of those who miss them, an indication of locale now appears as the first item in the annotation of each scene.

In the interest of both elegance and utility, each speech prefix is set in a separate line when the speaker's lines are in verse, except when those words form the second half of a verse line. Thus the verse form of the speech is kept visually intact. What is printed as verse and what is printed as prose has, in general, the authority of the original texts. Departures from the original texts in this regard have only the authority of editorial tradition and the judgment of the Pelican editors; and, in a few instances, are admittedly arbitrary.

The Theatrical World

ECONOMIC REALITIES determined the theatrical world in which Shakespeare's plays were written, performed, and received. For centuries in England, the primary theatrical tradition was nonprofessional. Craft guilds (or "mysteries") provided religious drama – mystery plays – as part of the celebration of religious and civic festivals, and schools and universities staged classical and neoclassical drama in both Latin and English as part of their curricula. In these forms, drama was established and socially acceptable. Professional theater, in contrast, existed on the margins of society. The acting companies were itinerant; playhouses could be any available space – the great halls of the aristocracy, town squares, civic halls, inn yards, fair booths, or open fields – and income was sporadic, dependent on the passing of the hat or on the bounty of local patrons. The actors, moreover, were considered little better than vagabonds, constantly in danger of arrest or expulsion.

In the late 1560s and 1570s, however, English professional theater began to gain respectability. Wealthy aristocrats fond of drama – the Lord Admiral, for example, or the Lord Chamberlain – took acting companies under their protection so that the players technically became members of their households and were no longer subject to arrest as homeless or masterless men. Permanent theaters were first built at this time as well, allowing the companies to control and charge for entry to their performances.

Shakespeare's livelihood, and the stunning artistic explosion in which he participated, depended on pragmatic and architectural effort. Professional theater requires ways to restrict access to its offerings; if it does not, and admission fees cannot be charged, the actors do not get paid, the costumes go to a pawnbroker, and there is no such thing as a professional, ongoing theatrical tradition. The answer to that economic need arrived in the late 1560s and 1570s with the creation of the so-called public or amphitheater playhouse. Recent discoveries indicate that the precursor of the Globe playhouse in London (where Shakespeare's mature plays were presented) and the Rose theater (which presented Christopher Marlowe's plays and some of Shakespeare's earliest ones) was the Red Lion theater of 1567. Archaeological studies of the foundations of the Rose and Globe theaters have revealed that the open-air theater of the 1590s and later was probably a polygonal building with fourteen to twenty or twenty-four sides, multistoried, from 75 to 100 feet in diameter, with a raised, partly covered "thrust" stage that projected into a group of standing patrons, or "groundlings," and a covered gallery, seating up to 2,500 or more (very crowded) spectators.

These theaters might have been about half full on any given day, though the audiences were larger on holidays or when a play was advertised, as old and new were, through printed playbills posted around London. The metropolitan area's late-Tudor, early-Stuart population (circa 1590–1620) has been estimated at about 150,000–250,000. It has been supposed that in the mid-1590s there were about 15,000 spectators per week at the public theaters; thus, as many as 10 percent of the local population went to the theater regularly. Consequently, the theaters' repertories – the plays available for this experienced and frequent audience – had to change often: in the month between September 15 and October 15, 1595, for instance, the Lord Admiral's Men performed twenty-eight times in eighteen different plays.

Since natural light illuminated the amphitheaters' stages, performances began between noon and two o'clock and ran without a break for two or three hours. They often concluded with a jig, a fencing display, or some other nondramatic exhibition. Weather conditions deter-

mined the season for the amphitheaters: plays were performed every day (including Sundays, sometimes, to clerical dismay) except during Lent – the forty days before
Easter – or periods of plague, or sometimes during the
summer months when law courts were not in session and
the most affluent members of the audience were not in
London.

To a modern theatergoer, an amphitheater stage like
that of the Rose or Globe would appear an unfamiliar mix-
ture of plainness and elaborate decoration. Much of the
structure was carved or painted, sometimes to imitate
marble; elsewhere, as under the canopy projecting over the
stage, to represent the stars and the zodiac. Appropriate
painted canvas pictures (of Jerusalem, for example, if the
play was set in that city) were apparently hung on the wall
behind the acting area, and tragedies were accompanied by
black hangings, presumably something like crepe festoons
or bunting. Although these theaters did not employ what
we would call scenery, early modern spectators saw numerous large props, such as the "bar" at which a prisoner stood
during a trial, the "mossy bank" where lovers reclined,
an arbor for amorous conversation, a chariot, gallows,
tables, trees, beds, thrones, writing desks, and so forth.
Audiences might learn a scene's location from a sign (reading "Athens," for example) carried across the stage (as in
Bertolt Brecht's twentieth-century productions). Equally
captivating (and equally irritating to the theater's enemies)
were the rich costumes and personal props the actors used:
the most valuable items in the surviving theatrical inven-
tories are the swords, gowns, robes, crowns, and other items
worn or carried by the performers.

Magic appealed to Shakespeare's audiences as much as
it does to us today, and the theater exploited many decep-
tive and spectacular devices. A winch in the loft above the
stage, called "the heavens," could lower and raise actors
playing gods, goddesses, and other supernatural figures to
and from the main acting area, just as one or more trap-
doors permitted entrances and exits to and from the area,

called "hell," beneath the stage. Actors wore elementary makeup such as wigs, false beards, and face paint, and they employed pig's bladders filled with animal blood to make wounds seem more real. They had rudimentary but effective ways of pretending to behead or hang a person. Supernumeraries (stagehands or actors not needed in a particular scene) could make thunder sounds (by shaking a metal sheet or rolling an iron ball down a chute) and show lightning (by blowing inflammable resin through tubes into a flame). Elaborate fireworks enhanced the effects of dragons flying through the air or imitated such celestial phenomena as comets, shooting stars, and multiple suns. Horses' hoofbeats, bells (located perhaps in the tower above the stage), trumpets and drums, clocks, cannon shots and gunshots, and the like were common sound effects. And the music of viols, cornets, oboes, and recorders was a regular feature of theatrical performances.

For two relatively brief spans, from the late 1570s to 1590 and from 1599 to 1614, the amphitheaters competed with the so-called private, or indoor, theaters, which originated as, or later represented themselves as, educational institutions training boys as singers for church services and court performances. These indoor theaters had two features that were distinct from the amphitheaters': their personnel and their playing spaces. The amphitheaters' adult companies included both adult men, who played the male roles, and boys, who played the female roles; the private, or indoor, theater companies, on the other hand, were entirely composed of boys aged about 8 to 16, who were, or could pretend to be, candidates for singers in a church or a royal boys' choir. (Until 1660, professional theatrical companies included no women.) The playing space would appear much more familiar to modern audiences than the long-vanished amphitheaters; the later indoor theaters were, in fact, the ancestors of the typical modern theater. They were enclosed spaces, usually rectangular, with the stage filling one end of the rectangle and the audience arrayed in seats or benches across (and sometimes lining) the building's longer axis. These spaces staged plays less frequently than the public theaters (perhaps only once a week) and held far fewer spectators than the amphitheaters: about 200 to 600, as opposed to 2,500 or more. Fewer patrons mean a smaller gross income, unless each pays more. Not surprisingly, then, private theaters charged higher prices than the amphitheaters, probably sixpence, as opposed to a penny for the cheapest entry.

Protected from the weather, the indoor theaters presented plays later in the day than the amphitheaters, and used artificial illumination – candles in sconces or candelabra. But candles melt, and need replacing, snuffing, and trimming, and these practical requirements may have been part of the reason the indoor theaters introduced breaks in the performance, the intermission so dear to the heart of theatergoers and to the pocketbooks of theater concessionaires ever since. Whether motivated by the need to tend to the candles or by the entrepreneurs' wishing to sell oranges and liquor, or both, the indoor theaters eventually established the modern convention of the non-continuous performance. In the early modern "private" theater, musical performances apparently filled the intermissions, which in Stuart theater jargon seem to have been called "acts."

At the end of the first decade of the seventeenth century, the distinction between public amphitheaters and private indoor companies ceased. For various cultural, political, and economic reasons, individual companies gained control of both the public, open-air theaters and the indoor ones, and companies mixing adult men and boys took over the formerly "private" theaters. Despite the death of the boys' companies and of their highly innovative theaters (for which such luminous playwrights as Ben Jonson, George Chapman, and John Marston wrote), their playing spaces and conventions had an immense impact on subsequent plays: not merely for the intervals (which stressed the artistic and architectonic importance of "acts"), but also because they introduced political and social satire as a popular dramatic ingredient, even in tragedy, and a wider range of actorly effects, encouraged by their more intimate playing spaces.

Even the briefest sketch of the Shakespearean theatrical world would be incomplete without some comment on the social and cultural dimensions of theaters and playing in the period. In an intensely hierarchical and status-conscious society, professional actors and their ventures had hardly any respectability; as we have indicated, to protect themselves against laws designed to curb vagabondage and the increase of masterless men, actors resorted to the near-fiction that they were the servants of noble masters, and wore their distinctive livery. Hence the company for which Shakespeare wrote in the 1590s called itself the Lord Chamberlain's Men and pretended that the public, money-getting performances were in fact rehearsals for private performances before that high court official. From 1598, the Privy Council had licensed theatrical companies, and after 1603, with the accession of King James I, the companies gained explicit royal protection, just as the Queen's Men had for a time under Queen Elizabeth. The Chamberlain's Men became the King's Men, and the other companies were patronized by the other members of the royal family.

These designations were legal fictions that half-concealed an important economic and social development, the evolution away from the theater's organization on the model of the guild, a self-regulating confraternity of individual artisans, into a proto-capitalist organization. Shakespeare's company became a joint-stock company, where persons who supplied capital and, in some cases, such as Shakespeare's, capital and talent, employed themselves and others in earning a return on that capital. This development meant that actors and theater companies were outside both the traditional guild structures, which required some form of civic or royal charter, and the feudal household organization of master-and-servant. This anomalous, maverick social and economic condition made theater companies practically unruly and poten-tially even dangerous; consequently, numerous official bodies – including the London metropolitan and ecclesi-astical authorities as well as, occasionally, the royal court itself – tried, without much success, to control and even to disband them.

Public officials had good reason to want to close the theaters: they were attractive nuisances – they drew often riotous crowds, they were always noisy, and they could be politically offensive and socially insubordinate. Until the Civil War, however, anti-theatrical forces failed to shut down professional theater, for many reasons – limited surveillance and few police powers, tensions or outright hostilities among the agencies that sought to check or channel theatrical activity, and lack of clear policies for control. Another reason must have been the theaters' un-deniable popularity. Curtailing any activity enjoyed by such a substantial percentage of the population was diffi-cult, as various Roman emperors attempting to limit cir-cuses had learned, and the Tudor-Stuart audience was not merely large, it was socially diverse and included women. The prevalence of public entertainment in this period has been underestimated. In fact, fairs, holidays, games, sporting events, the equivalent of modern parades, freak shows, and street exhibitions all abounded, but the the-ater was the most widely and frequently available enter-tainment to which people of every class had access. That fact helps account both for its quantity and for the fear and anger it aroused.

WILLIAM SHAKESPEARE OF STRATFORD-UPON-AVON, GENTLEMAN

Many people have said that we know very little about William Shakespeare's life – pinheads and postcards are often mentioned as appropriately tiny surfaces on which to record the available information. More imaginatively and perhaps more correctly, Ralph Waldo Emerson wrote, "Shakespeare is the only biographer of Shakespeare. . . . So far from Shakespeare's being the least known, he is the one person in all modern history fully known to us."

In fact, we know more about Shakespeare's life than we do about almost any other English writer's of his era. His last will and testament (dated March 25, 1616) survives, as do numerous legal contracts and court documents involving Shakespeare as principal or witness, and parish records in Stratford and London. Shakespeare appears quite often in official records of King James's royal court, and of course Shakespeare's name appears on numerous title pages and in the written and recorded words of his literary contemporaries Robert Greene, Henry Chettle, Francis Meres, John Davies of Hereford, Ben Jonson, and many others. Indeed, if we make due allowance for the bloating of modern, run-of-the-mill bureaucratic records, more information has survived over the past four hundred years about William Shakespeare of Stratford-upon-Avon, Warwickshire, than is likely to survive in the next four hundred years about any reader of these words.

What we do not have are entire categories of information – Shakespeare's private letters or diaries, drafts and revisions of poems and plays, critical prefaces or essays, commendatory verse for other writers' works, or instructions guiding his fellow actors in their performances, for instance – that we imagine would help us understand and appreciate his surviving writings. For all we know, many such data never existed as written records. Many literary and theatrical critics, not knowing what might once have existed, more or less cheerfully accept the situation; some even make a theoretical virtue of it by claiming that such data are irrelevant to understanding and interpreting the plays and poems.

So, what do we know about William Shakespeare, the man responsible for thirty-seven or perhaps more plays, more than 150 sonnets, two lengthy narrative poems, and some shorter poems?

While many families by the name of Shakespeare (or some variant spelling) can be identified in the English Midlands as far back as the twelfth century, it seems likely that the dramatist's grandfather, Richard, moved to Snitterfield, a town not far from Stratford-upon-Avon, sometime before 1529. In Snitterfield, Richard Shakespeare leased farmland from the very wealthy Robert Arden. By 1552, Richard's son John had moved to a large house on Henley Street in Stratford-upon-Avon, the house that stands today as "The Birthplace." In Stratford, John Shakespeare traded as a glover, dealt in wool, and lent money at interest; he also served in a variety of civic posts, including "High Bailiff," the municipality's equivalent of mayor. In 1557, he married Robert Arden's youngest daughter, Mary. Mary and John had four sons – William was the oldest – and four daughters, of whom only Joan outlived her most celebrated sibling. William was baptized (an event entered in the Stratford parish church records) on April 26, 1564, and it has become customary, without any good factual support, to suppose he was born on April 23, which happens to be the feast day of Saint George, patron saint of England, and is also the date on which he died, in 1616. Shakespeare married Anne Hathaway in 1582, when he was eighteen and she was twenty-six; their first child was born five months later. It has been generally assumed that the marriage was enforced and subsequently unhappy, but these are only assumptions; it has been estimated, for instance, that up to one third of Elizabethan brides were pregnant when they married. Anne and William Shakespeare had three children: Susanna, who married a prominent local physician, John Hall; and the twins Hamnet, who died young in 1596, and Judith, who married Thomas Quiney – apparently a rather shady individual. The name Hamnet was unusual but not unique: he and his twin sister were named for their godparents, Shakespeare's neighbors Hamnet and Judith Sadler. Shakespeare's father died in 1601 (the year of *Hamlet*), and Mary Arden Shakespeare died in 1608 (the year of *Coriolanus*). William Shakespeare's last surviving direct descendant was his granddaughter Elizabeth Hall, who died in 1670.

Between the birth of the twins in 1585 and a clear reference to Shakespeare as a practicing London dramatist in Robert Greene's sensationalizing, satiric pamphlet, *Greene's Groatsworth of Wit* (1592), there is no record of where William Shakespeare was or what he was doing. These seven so-called lost years have been imaginatively filled by scholars and other students of Shakespeare: some think he traveled to Italy, or fought in the Low Countries, or studied law or medicine, or worked as an apprentice actor/writer, and so on to even more fanciful possibilities. Whatever the biographical facts for those "lost" years, Greene's nasty remarks in 1592 testify to professional envy and to the fact that Shakespeare already had a successful career in London. Speaking to his fellow playwrights, Greene warns both generally and specifically:

> . . . trust them [actors] not: for there is an upstart crow, beautified with our feathers, that with his tiger's heart wrapped in a player's hide supposes he is as well able to bombast out a blank verse as the best of you; and being an absolute Johannes Factotum, is in his own conceit the only Shake-scene in a country.

The passage mimics a line from *3 Henry VI* (hence the play must have been performed before Greene wrote) and seems to say that "Shake-scene" is both actor and playwright, a jack-of-all-trades. That same year, Henry Chettle protested Greene's remarks in *Kind-Heart's Dream,* and each of the next two years saw the publication of poems – *Venus and Adonis* and *The Rape of Lucrece,* respectively – publicly ascribed to (and dedicated by) Shakespeare. Early in 1595 he was named one of the senior members of a prominent acting company, the Lord Chamberlain's Men, when they received payment for court performances during the 1594 Christmas season.

Clearly, Shakespeare had achieved both success and reputation in London. In 1596, upon Shakespeare's application, the College of Arms granted his father the now-familiar coat of arms he had taken the first steps to obtain almost twenty years before, and in 1598, John's son – now permitted to call himself "gentleman" – took a 10 percent share in the new Globe playhouse. In 1597, he bought a substantial bourgeois house, called New Place, in Stratford – the garden remains, but Shakespeare's house, several times rebuilt, was torn down in 1759 – and over the next few years Shakespeare spent large sums buying land and making other investments in the town and its environs. Though he worked in London, his family remained in Stratford, and he seems always to have considered Stratford the home he would eventually return to. Something approaching a disinterested appreciation of Shakespeare's popular and professional status appears in Francis Meres's *Palladis Tamia* (1598), a not especially imaginative and perhaps therefore persuasive record of literary reputations. Reviewing contemporary English writers, Meres lists the titles of many of Shakespeare's plays, including one not now known, *Love's Labor's Won,* and praises his "mellifluous & hony-tongued" "sugred Sonnets," which were then circulating in manuscript (they were first collected in 1609). Meres describes Shakespeare as "one of the best" English playwrights of both comedy and tragedy. In *Remains . . . Concerning Britain* (1605), William Camden – a more authoritative source than the imitative Meres – calls Shakespeare one of the "most pregnant witts of these our times" and joins him with such writers as Chapman, Daniel, Jonson, Marston, and Spenser. During the first decades of the seventeenth century, publishers began to attribute numerous play quartos, including some non-Shakespearean ones, to Shakespeare, either by name or initials, and we may assume that they deemed Shakespeare's name and supposed authorship, true or false, commercially attractive.

For the next ten years or so, various records show

Shakespeare's dual career as playwright and man of the theater in London, and as an important local figure in Stratford. In 1608-9 his acting company – designated the "King's Men" soon after King James had succeeded Queen Elizabeth in 1603 – rented, refurbished, and opened a small interior playing space, the Blackfriars theater, in London, and Shakespeare was once again listed as a substantial sharer in the group of proprietors of the playhouse. By May 11, 1612, however, he describes himself as a Stratford resident in a London lawsuit – an indication that he had withdrawn from day-to-day professional activity and returned to the town where he had always had his main financial interests. When Shakespeare bought a substantial residential building in London, the Blackfriars Gatehouse, close to the theater of the same name, on March 10, 1613, he is recorded as William Shakespeare "of Stratford upon Avon in the county of Warwick, gentleman," and he named several London residents as the building's trustees. Still, he continued to participate in theatrical activity: when the new Earl of Rutland needed an allegorical design to bear as a shield, or *impresa*, at the celebration of King James's Accession Day, March 24, 1613, the earl's accountant recorded a payment of 44 shillings to Shakespeare for the device with its motto.

For the last few years of his life, Shakespeare evidently concentrated his activities in the town of his birth. Most of the final records concern business transactions in Stratford, ending with the notation of his death on April 23, 1616, and burial in Holy Trinity Church, Stratford-upon-Avon.

THE QUESTION OF AUTHORSHIP

The history of ascribing Shakespeare's plays (the poems do not come up so often) to someone else began, as it continues, peculiarly. The earliest published claim that someone else wrote Shakespeare's plays appeared in an 1856 article by Delia Bacon in the American journal *Putnam's Monthly* – although an Englishman, Thomas Wilmot, had shared his doubts in private (even secretive) conversations with friends near the end of the eighteenth century. Bacon's was a sad personal history that ended in madness and poverty, but the year after her article, she published, with great difficulty and the bemused assistance of Nathaniel Hawthorne (then United States Consul in Liverpool, England), her *Philosophy of the Plays of Shakspere Unfolded*. This huge, ornately written, confusing farrago is almost unreadable; sometimes its intents, to say nothing of its arguments, disappear entirely beneath near-raving, ecstatic writing. Tumbled in with much supposed "philosophy" appear the claims that Francis Bacon (from whom Delia Bacon eventually claimed descent), Walter Ralegh, and several other contemporaries of Shakespeare's had written the plays. The book had little impact except as a ridiculed curiosity.

Once proposed, however, the issue gained momentum among people whose conviction was the greater in proportion to their ignorance of sixteenth- and seventeenth-century English literature, history, and society. Another American amateur, Catherine P. Ashmead Windle, made the next influential contribution to the cause when she published *Report to the British Museum* (1882), wherein she promised to open "the Cipher of Francis Bacon," though what she mostly offers, in the words of S. Schoenbaum, is "demented allegorizing." An entire new cottage industry grew from Windle's suggestion that the texts contain hidden, cryptographically discoverable ciphers – "clues" – to their authorship; and today there are not only books devoted to the putative ciphers, but also pamphlets, journals, and newsletters.

Although Baconians have led the pack of those seeking a substitute Shakespeare, in *"Shakespeare" Identified* (1920), J. Thomas Looney became the first published

"Oxfordian" when he proposed Edward de Vere, seventeenth earl of Oxford, as the secret author of Shakespeare's plays. Also for Oxford and his "authorship" there are today dedicated societies, articles, journals, and books. Less popular candidates – Queen Elizabeth and Christopher Marlowe among them – have had adherents, but the movement seems to have divided into two main contending factions, Baconian and Oxfordian. (For further details on all the candidates for "Shakespeare," see S. Schoenbaum, *Shakespeare's Lives,* 2nd ed., 1991.)

The Baconians, the Oxfordians, and supporters of other candidates have one trait in common – they are snobs. Every pro-Bacon or pro-Oxford tract sooner or later claims that the historical William Shakespeare of Stratford-upon-Avon could not have written the plays because he could not have had the training, the university education, the experience, and indeed the imagination or background their author supposedly possessed. Only a learned genius like Bacon or an aristocrat like Oxford could have written such fine plays. (As it happens, lucky male children of the middle class had access to better education than most aristocrats in Elizabethan England – and Oxford was not particularly well educated.) Shakespeare received in the Stratford grammar school a formal education that would daunt many college graduates today; and popular rival playwrights such as the very learned Ben Jonson and George Chapman, both of whom also lacked university training, achieved great artistic success, without being taken as Bacon or Oxford.

Besides snobbery, one other quality characterizes the authorship controversy: lack of evidence. A great deal of testimony from Shakespeare's time shows that Shakespeare wrote Shakespeare's plays and that his contemporaries recognized them as distinctive and distinctly superior. (Some of that contemporary evidence is collected in E. K. Chambers, *William Shakespeare: A Study of Facts and Problems,* 2 vols., 1930.) Since that testimony comes from Shakespeare's enemies and theatrical competitors as well as from his co-workers and from the Elizabethan equivalent of literary journalists, it seems unlikely that, if any one of these sources had known he was a fraud, they would have failed to record that fact.

Books About Shakespeare's Theater

Useful scholarly studies of theatrical life in Shakespeare's day include: G. E. Bentley, *The Jacobean and Caroline Stage,* 7 vols. (1941-68), and the same author's *The Professions of Dramatist and Player in Shakespeare's Time, 1590-1642* (1986); E. K. Chambers, *The Elizabethan Stage,* 4 vols. (1923); R. A. Foakes, *Illustrations of the English Stage, 1580-1642* (1985); Andrew Gurr, *The Shakespearean Stage,* 3rd ed. (1992), and the same author's *Play-going in Shakespeare's London,* 2nd ed. (1996); Edwin Nungezer, *A Dictionary of Actors* (1929); Carol Chillington Rutter, ed., *Documents of the Rose Playhouse* (1984).

Books About Shakespeare's Life

The following books provide scholarly, documented accounts of Shakespeare's life: G. E. Bentley, *Shakespeare: A Biographical Handbook* (1961); E. K. Chambers, *William Shakespeare: A Study of Facts and Problems,* 2 vols. (1930); S. Schoenbaum, *William Shakespeare: A Compact Documentary Life* (1977); and *Shakespeare's Lives,* 2nd ed. (1991), by the same author. Many scholarly editions of Shakespeare's complete works print brief compilations of essential dates and events. References to Shakespeare's works up to 1700 are collected in C. M. Ingleby et al., *The Shakespeare Allusion-Book,* rev. ed., 2 vols. (1932).

The Texts of Shakespeare

As FAR AS WE KNOW, only one manuscript conceivably in Shakespeare's own hand may (and even this is much disputed) exist: a few pages of a play called *Sir Thomas More*, which apparently was never performed. What we do have, as later readers, performers, scholars, students, are printed texts. The earliest of these survive in two forms: quartos and folios. Quartos (from the Latin for "four") are small books, printed on sheets of paper that were then folded in fours, to make eight double-sided pages. When these were bound together, the result was a squarish, eminently portable volume that sold for the relatively small sum of sixpence (translating in modern terms to about $5.00). In folios, on the other hand, the sheets are folded only once, in half, producing large, impressive volumes taller than they are wide. This was the format for important works of philosophy, science, theology, and literature (the major precedent for a folio Shakespeare was Ben Jonson's *Works*, 1616). The decision to print the works of a popular playwright in folio is an indication of how far up on the social scale the theatrical profession had come during Shakespeare's lifetime. The Shakespeare folio was an expensive book, selling for between fifteen and eighteen shillings, depending on the binding (in modern terms, from about $150 to $180). Twenty Shakespeare plays of the thirty-seven that survive first appeared in quarto, seventeen of which appeared during Shakespeare's lifetime; the rest of the plays are found only in folio.

The First Folio was published in 1623, seven years after Shakespeare's death, and was authorized by his fellow actors, the co-owners of the King's Men. This publication was certainly a mark of the company's enormous respect for Shakespeare; but it was also a way of turning the old plays, most of which were no longer current in the play-house, into ready money (the folio includes only Shake-speare's plays, not his sonnets or other nondramatic verse). Whatever the motives behind the publication of the folio, the texts it preserves constitute the basis for almost all later editions of the playwright's works. The texts, however, differ from those of the earlier quartos, sometimes in minor respects but often significantly – most strikingly in the two texts of *King Lear*, but also in important ways in *Hamlet, Othello,* and *Troilus and Cressida.* (The variants are recorded in the textual notes to each play in the new Pelican series.) The differences in these texts represent, in a sense, the essence of theater: the texts of plays were initially not intended for publication. They were scripts, designed for the actors to perform – the principal life of the play at this period was in performance. And it follows that in Shakespeare's theater the playwright typically had no say either in how his play was performed or in the disposition of his text – he was an employee of the company. The authoritative figures in the theatrical enterprise were the shareholders in the company, who were for the most part the major actors. They decided what plays were to be done; they hired the playwright and often gave him an outline of the play they wanted him to write. Often, too, the play was a collaboration: the company would retain a group of writers, and parcel out the scenes among them. The resulting script was then the property of the company, and the actors would revise it as they saw fit during the course of putting it on stage. The resulting text belonged to the company. The playwright had no rights in it once he had been paid. (This system survives largely intact in the movie industry, and most of the playwrights of Shakespeare's time were as anonymous as most screenwriters are today.) The script could also, of course, continue to change as the tastes of audiences and the requirements of the actors changed. Many – perhaps most – plays were revised when they were reintroduced after any substantial absence from the repertory, or when they were performed by a company different from the one that originally commissioned the play.

Shakespeare was an exceptional figure in this world because he was not only a shareholder and actor in his company, but also its leading playwright – he was literally his own boss. He had, moreover, little interest in the publication of his plays, and even those that appeared during his lifetime with the authorization of the company show no signs of any editorial concern on the part of the author. Theater was, for Shakespeare, a fluid and supremely responsive medium – the very opposite of the great classic canonical text that has embodied his works since 1623.

The very fluidity of the original texts, however, has meant that Shakespeare has always had to be edited. Here is an example of how problematic the editorial project inevitably is, a passage from the most famous speech in *Romeo and Juliet,* Juliet's balcony soliloquy beginning "O Romeo, Romeo, wherefore art thou Romeo?" Since the eighteenth century, the standard modern text has read,

> What's Montague? It is nor hand, nor foot,
> Nor arm, nor face, nor any other part
> Belonging to a man. O be some other name!
> What's in a name? That which we call a rose
> By any other name would smell as sweet.
>
> (II.2.40–44)

Editors have three early texts of this play to work from, two quarto texts and the folio. Here is how the First Quarto (1597) reads:

> Whats *Mountague?* It is nor hand nor foote,
> Nor arme, nor face, nor any other part.
> Whats in a name? That which we call a Rofe,
> By any other name would fmell as fweet:

Here is the Second Quarto (1599):

Whats *Mountague*? it is nor hand nor foote,
Nor arme nor face, ô be some other name
Belonging to a man.
Whats in a name that which we call a rose,
By any other word would smell as sweete,

And here is the First Folio (1623):

What's *Mountague*? it is nor hand nor foote,
Nor arme, nor face, O be some other name
Belonging to a man.
What? in a names that which we call a Rose,
By any other word would smell as sweete,

There is in fact no early text that reads as our modern text does – and this is the most famous speech in the play. Instead, we have three quite different texts, all of which are clearly some version of the same speech, but none of which seems to us a final or satisfactory version. The transcendently beautiful passage in modern editions is an editorial invention: editors have succeeded in conflating and revising the three versions into something we recognize as great poetry. Is this what Shakespeare "really" wrote? Who can say? What we can say is that Shakespeare always had performance, not a book, in mind.

Books About the Shakespeare Texts

The standard study of the printing history of the First Folio is W. W. Greg, *The Shakespeare First Folio* (1955). J. K. Walton, *The Quarto Copy for the First Folio of Shakespeare* (1971), is a useful survey of the relation of the quartos to the folio. The second edition of Charlton Hinman's *Norton Facsimile* of the First Folio (1996), with a new introduction by Peter Blayney, is indispensable. Stanley Wells and Gary Taylor, *William Shakespeare: A Textual Companion*, keyed to the Oxford text, gives a comprehensive survey of the editorial situation for all the plays and poems.

THE GENERAL EDITORS

Introduction

*H*ENRY *V* IS BOTH the capstone and the keystone of Shakespeare's engagement with the English history play. First printed as a quarto in 1600, it is the ninth and final play on English history he wrote in the 1590s. It closes the "second tetralogy" of history plays (*Richard II, 1* and *2 Henry IV,* and *Henry V*), those plays that Shakespeare wrote following the "first tetralogy," four plays about the Wars of the Roses (*1, 2,* and *3 Henry VI* and *Richard III*). Narratively and in historical chronology, however, *Henry V* occupies the midpoint and offers a pause in the fifteenth-century civil conflicts inaugurated by the overthrow (1399) of Richard II by Henry IV and concluded by the defeat (1485) of Richard III by Henry Tudor. *Henry V* thus portrays a high, and perhaps unique, moment in English national history, when it represents a country both internally unified and internationally victorious, one that has briefly exchanged civil unrest for foreign triumph: "Small time; but in that small most greatly lived / This Star of England" (Epilogue, 5-6). Henry was a king of legendary repute, and his story would have been available to Shakespeare not only in the chronicle histories of Hall and Holinshed, but also in the anonymous play *The Famous Victories of Henry V* (registered for publication in 1594 and printed in 1598). Coming as it does at the end of the 1590s, a decade after Elizabethan England's own improbable triumph over the Spanish Armada (1588), and a decade increasingly beset by sectarian division under an aging monarch without an acknowledged successor, Shakespeare's play resurrects a medieval moment of English triumph to represent a climax both of patriotism and of Shakespeare's historical dramaturgy.

If in the *Henry IV* plays a central concern was the creation of a political ruler, in *Henry V* the emphasis shifts to the creation of political community under that ruler. In his last words to his prodigal son, Henry IV urged him to "busy giddy minds with foreign quarrels," and in this play King Henry V takes that advice to heart by embarking on war with France under the guise of reclaiming England's hereditary rights thereto. The result is a nation unified, however temporarily and tenuously, by the presence of a foreign enemy. As if to mirror the sentiment of unity, Shakespeare includes players from all walks of war: the ruler and his backroom policymakers, officers and common soldiers, even camp followers have their moment at center stage. A similar treatment is afforded the enemy as well.

Patriotism, however, is a complicated experience, and nowhere more than in this evocation. The play is both a story of rapacious warfare and a romantic comedy; England is both underdog and aggressor; unified and fractious; a "band of brothers" and an army with a strict, and strictly enforced, pecking order. Henry himself is both the "mirror of all Christian kings" and a ruthless and Machiavellian performer of power. Near the play's conclusion, Burgundy, brokering political peace through the royal marriage of Henry with Katherine of France, invokes the image of the anamorph, a figure that produces two different images from two different perspectives, in order to answer Henry's warning that he "cannot see many a fair French city for one fair French maid that stands in my way": "Yes, my lord, you see them perspectively, the cities turned into a maid" (V.2.315-17). This equivalence of female and territorial bodies occurs several times in the play, as violence is transformed into romance, and vice versa (Henry's threat to rape and pillage the town of Harfleur, for instance, is followed by a scene in which Katherine learns English names for parts of her body). Perhaps anamorphism best sums up the curious compound of perspectives – romance and realpolitik – that constitutes this play.

Structurally, Shakespeare signals this contrast between ideal and real perspectives on political community through using a chorus to frame the action. The Chorus, a relatively rare feature of Shakespeare's dramaturgy, is here relentlessly optimistic and positive in presenting future events, while the scenes that follow the Chorus's appearances persistently contradict or qualify that idealization. The first chorus, for instance, speaks in glorious terms of the "warlike Harry," who will "Assume the port of Mars, and at his heels, / Leashed in like hounds, should famine, sword, and fire / Crouch for employment" (Prologue 5-8). The opening scenes, however, depict the clergy scheming to support international warfare in order to protect church property, and a king eager for ecclesiastical and legal sanction of what is more murkily a war of territorial expansion. When delivered, the clerical sanction is neither clear nor necessarily righteous: the Salic law speech by the Archbishop of Canterbury constitutes a moment of high antiquarian comedy. To muddy the issue further, Henry's motives are not free from personal pique: far from assuming the port of Mars, he must parry a mocking challenge from the enemy, in the form of a gift of tennis balls, reminding him of his former "wilder days" (I.2.268). Right from the outset, Shakespeare presents us with a competition among interpretations, motives, and rationales for the undertaking he is about to represent.

This contrast persists in the subsequent pairings of chorus and action: in the second chorus, we hear that "all the youth of England are on fire" (II.Cho.1), only to be confronted with the spectacle of Nym and Pistol quarreling nearly to blows over the dubious favors of Mistress Quickly; they are on fire, but less with a burning zeal for military glory than the potential sores of the pox. Similarly, the third chorus urges upon us the glory of embarkation for France and the bravery of "culled and choice-drawn cavaliers"; what follows is the ignominious spectacle of Nym, Bardolph, and Pistol having to be cudgeled into combat by Fluellen. As the Boy wryly com-

ments, "three such antics do not amount to a man"
(III.2.30). And so on and so forth. It is not just the former tavern denizens who deflate the epic tones. The
"main intendment of the Scot" to invade England while
her armies are occupied abroad, the squabbling among
the four captains meant to convey the unity of Britain,
the dispute between the king and the common soldier
Williams, between Fluellen and Pistol, the vanity of the
French camp – all serve to sully the romance of war, and
make hollow the promise of a country unified by whatever means.

But if Shakespeare refuses to let the ideal vision of warfare and national unity stand unmolested, at the same
time he insists, in an inspiring and rousing rhetoric, on
the ennobling capacities of participation in a myth of
unity and union. The first chorus appeals to the audience
as if it were collectively ennobled by this enterprise, "gentles all": "For 'tis your thoughts that now must deck our
kings" (Prologue 28). This double register is nowhere so
present as in the language of the king himself. Henry produces what is undoubtedly among the most spine-tin-
gling of calls to battle in Shakespeare or anywhere else. In
his Saint Crispin's Day speech before the battle, Henry
proffers a fantasy of national unity to his company: "We
few, we happy few, we band of brothers; / For he today
that sheds his blood with me / Shall be my brother. Be he
ne'er so vile, / This day shall gentle his condition"
(IV.3.61-64). The words are thrilling and inspiring, as
they are intended to be. Yet in death, on the very heels of
the battle, this brotherhood is coldly enumerated by
Henry not as a single fellowship but in order of rank and
degree (IV.8.90-102). Throughout the play Henry speaks
in many voices: he threatens war and rapine, as in the
speech before the gates of Harfleur – "the fleshed soldier,
rough and hard of heart, / In liberty of bloody hand shall
range / With conscience wide as hell, mowing like grass /
Your fresh fair virgins and your flow'ring infants"
(III.3.11-14). But he also condemns them, as when he re-

fuses to pardon a thieving Bardolph: "We would have all such offenders so cut off. And we give express charge that in our marches through the country there be nothing compelled from the villages, nothing taken but paid for; . . . for when lenity and cruelty play for a kingdom, the gentler gamester is the soonest winner" (III.6.104-10). This king can both rouse and douse, stir and squelch, rally and cavil. Henry's own speech thus mimics the double register elaborated structurally in the play.

These two sides – the inspiring and the calculating – constitute the double face of Henry, but it is a duality that does not so much discredit his rulership as render it all the more compelling. He is both righteous and ruthless, glorious and repellent, and the combination serves to make him both difficult to grasp and a king for every moment. Part of his complexity is historical, for Henry comes with a reputation as a prodigal prince, one given in his youth, as Canterbury puts it, to "Hydra-headed willfulness" (I.1.35), but who upon ascending the throne demonstrates a nearly miraculous conversion to duty and the responsibilities of rule: "Consideration like an angel came / And whipped th' offending Adam out of him" (I.1.28-29). Glimpses and echoes of this roguish past are present throughout the play, in the motley tavern soldiers, in the Dauphin's jest, and in the account of the death of Falstaff and his ignominious memorial in Fluellen's report: "the fat knight with the great pelly doublet. He was full of jests, and gipes, and knaveries, and mocks. I have forgot his name" (IV.7.46-49). The episode where Henry disguises himself in order to circulate among his troops (IV.1) is perhaps the most reminiscent of his previous dissemblings.

Yet if Henry is shadowed by his former life of tavern-dwelling escapades, these ghosts do not so much fondly recall to us his claim to good fellowship – to "drink with any tinker in his own language," as he puts it in *1 Henry IV* (II.4) – as remind us of how different he now is, now that he has brutally and dramatically cast off old loyalties in order to make his own rule appear the more pure and powerful. The death of Falstaff from heartbreak, received only in report ("The king has killed his heart," II.1.85), is followed by Bardolph's death, and then by that of the engaging boy who follows the tavern crew to battle. It is as if bit by bit Henry's former career, and the image of good fellowship it promulgated, is being exterminated in the service of the king's new sanctity. Of these three deaths, it is the last alone, perhaps because it is the last, and the least, that draws a response from the king: "I was not angry since I came to France / Until this instant" (IV.7.54) – the dead boy is, it seems, the page Henry had once given Falstaff. The result is that we begin fondly to allow the image of Henry's common touch, but nostalgically only, as if we too realize the need to sacrifice such bonds (ironically enough) in the service of corporate statehood.

Of course, if memory serves correctly, Prince Hal was never *really* a good fellow, but only appeared so, and only as long as that image was useful to him. In *1 Henry IV* he spoke to us in soliloquy, revealing his "loose behavior" as a mere foil to his eventual "reformation," intended to render his ultimate conversion to duty all the more miraculous and compelling because so unexpected. Our sense of him then, and now, was above all as an *actor,* one who knew how to manipulate settings and scenes to his own advantage. In *Henry V,* this sense of his character as an actor of many roles persists, as his dexterity with multiple voices suggests. But it is no longer so self-conscious a performance, as if Henry himself has come to believe his own propaganda, or as if the sense of playful distance on his own identity was a luxury to be relinquished along with his tavern buddies. When we do see and hear him in soliloquy, that moment when an actor stands alone before an audience, and typically a moment of intimate confidence, he seems woefully sincere, and indeed ends by speaking to God in a prayer for absolution. Though he speaks of the merely mortal quality of a ruler – "what have kings that privates have not too, / Save ceremony, save general ceremony?" (IV.1.231-32) – the effect is less of a demystification of power than a whining complaint that it's lonely at the top. His closing plea to the heavens to "think not upon the fault / My father made in compassing the crown!" (IV.1.286-87) is startling in its filial disloyalty and the admission that royal power is more often brutally seized than divinely transferred. But Henry rapidly remystifies his own rule in distancing himself from such sordid wrangling: "I Richard's body have interrèd new; / And on it have bestowed more contrite tears / Than from it issued forcèd drops of blood" (IV.1.288-90). Whither irony? It seems as if the Henry who once understood and reveled in the facades of power dies when Falstaff's heart dies.

But true to the endless ebb and flow of this play's emotional tides, we are offered compensation for our loss. If Henry sheds his prodigal identity, he also acquires a new one, that of the rough and ready suitor of a French princess. Perhaps the most strongly idealizing movement of this play lies not in the imprecations of the Chorus to and for glory, but in its ultimate composition as a form of romantic comedy.

The Act V meeting between Henry and Katherine of France is one that is anticipated from Act III, scene 4, when we first meet Katherine as she learns English from her maid. Even as the audience knows to anticipate the ultimate union of France and England in marriage, this princess seems herself to anticipate her eventual meeting with Henry, as she asks her nurse for a language lesson in the tongue of her country's imminent conqueror: "il faut que j'apprends à parler" (III.4.4-5): it is necessary that I learn to speak [it]. Katherine seemingly knows in advance her destiny as an English queen. The comic momentum of this marriage, in which political contest will be resolved in personal union, is seconded in the content of this scene: Katherine learns English by learning to name the parts of her body, as if she knew that it is that very body, and its production of an heir to the English throne, that will provide the resolution of Henry's territorial claims to France. As Queen Isabel of France puts it, "As man and wife, being two, are one in love, / So be there 'twixt your kingdoms such a spousal" (V.2.357-58). The bawdy language of the princess acknowledges that a French body Englished is rendered a sexualized space; her words transpose to a comic key the aggressively political nature of the preceding scene, where Henry threatened Harfleur with rape and pillage, a vision of "pure maidens fall[ing] into the hand / Of hot and forcing violation" (III.3.20-21). Such is in fact the function of this royal marriage, to aestheticize and romanticize the brutality of foreign invasion, to convert rape into romance.

It is a potentially clumsy conversion, as Henry himself seems to realize in the wooing scene. Henry's final appearance before us is in the role of the self-admittedly ungainly suitor, "such a plain king that thou wouldst think I had sold my farm to buy my crown" (V.2.126-28). But of course if Henry is unaccomplished in love language, he is by no means at a loss for words. Here we see a hint of the Henry of old, the master of puns and double meanings, the most "comparative rascalliest sweet young prince," as Falstaff once termed him (*1 Henry IV,* I.2). This time of course his linguistic play, like her earlier bawdy translations, is at Katherine's expense: "Do you like me, Kate?" he asks, bluntly anglicizing her name. "Pardonnez-moi," she begs him, "I cannot tell wat is 'like me.'" "An angel is like you, Kate, and you are like an angel" (V.2.108-11). But no amount of gallantry can disguise the political content of this wooing, as Katherine herself shrewdly points out: "Is it possible dat I sould love de *ennemie* of France?" (169-70). It is a scene in which both parties baldly acknowledge the political work that romance must do, but that wins us nevertheless. Perhaps because we know this union is inevitable; Shakespeare takes a foregone conclusion of history and, "bending author" that he is, manages to give it a shapely comic turn. But also perhaps the scene charms us because we know its satisfactions to be short-lived. For however triumphant, militaristic, chauvinist, or glorifying of war and national unity this play may be, as the final chorus acknowledges, this celebration is also notoriously temporary. Henry V ruled for nine years only, and his son "in infant bands crowned king . . . / Whose state so many had the managing / That they lost France and made his England bleed" (Epi.9-12). For once, the Chorus speaks the deflating language of real consequences in stark contrast to the closing and triumphant harmonies of the wooing scene. It is a sobering conclusion, and a poignant one. The idealizing pressures of *Henry V* may at times cloy and coerce; but we ultimately forgive the play its glorifications, not only because we too crave a world where the underdog is the victor, few of the good guys die, and the hero gets the girl, but because we also know – and here we learn again – that such things are all too rare and fleeting.

CLAIRE MCEACHERN
University of California at Los Angeles

Note on the Text

THERE ARE TWO TEXTS with primary authority for *Henry V*: the quarto of 1600 and the folio of 1623. The quarto text, twice reprinted (1602, 1619), is not divided into acts and scenes; it lacks the six choruses, and some characters (e.g., Macmorris, Jamy, and the Dauphin – replaced by Bourbon) and scenes (e.g., I.1, III.1, IV.2). Q1 sets the entire play as verse. Editors generally imagine Q to be the printing of a memorial reconstruction of a text abridged for performance with a reduced cast, and it is thought that the two reporters of the text took the parts of Exeter and Gower, because scenes where those characters appear agree more fully with the folio version.

The folio forms the basis for the text of this edition and is thought to derive from Shakespeare's manuscript. In its original form it lacks blasphemous oaths (present, for instance, in Q, and presumably censored by the printers in accordance with the Act of 1606 to restrain the use of oaths in plays). Its division of acts differs from that imposed by editorial tradition (followed here: Acts I and II correspond to Act I of F; Act III to Act II; the first six scenes of Act IV to Act III; the remainder of Act IV to Act IV. Modern and F Act V are identical). The modern division is based on the position of the four internal speeches by the Chorus, although it is possible that the choruses have no formal significance.

The present edition modernizes spelling and punctuation, normalizes speech prefixes, and occasionally re-lineates the text of F (for instance, Pistol's speeches, which are printed as prose in F). Fluellen's Welsh dialect has been normalized by the consistent use of "orld" for "world," "Cheshu" for "Jesu," and "p" for initial "b" in stressed syllables. Contrary to general practice in modern editions of this play, the passages in French are no more extensively modified than the passages in English. Archaic and familiar grammatical forms, as well as errors in grammar and idiom (e.g., Henry's), have been retained.

The following is a complete list of all substantive departures from the text of the folio of 1623 (F). The adopted readings in italics from the quarto of 1600 (Q) and from the later folios and editors are followed by the folio readings in roman, except for stage directions (in italics).

I.2 38 *succedant* (F2) succedaul   45, 52 *Elbe* (Capell) Elue   74 *Lingard* (Sisson) Lingare   82 *Ermengard* (Sisson) Ermengare   94 *imbar* (F3) imbarre   131 *blood* (F3) Bloods   163 *her* (Capell) their   209 *many several* (Q) many   213 *End* (Q) And

II.1 22 *mare* (Q) name   26 *How . . . Pistol* (joined in F to preceding speech by Bardolph; assigned in Q to Nym)   39, 40 *Iceland* (Steevens) Island   69 *Coupe la* (Dyce) Couple a   70 *thee defy* (Q) defie thee   77 *enough.* (Pope) enough to   80 *you,* (Hanmer) your   111 *that's* (Q) that   113 *Ah* (Pope) A

II.2 75 *hath* (Q) have   87 *furnish him* (F2) furnish   108 *whoop* (Theobald) hoope   114 *All* (Hanmer) And   122 *lion gait* (Capell) Lyon-gate   139 *mark the* (Malone) make thee   147 *Henry* (Q) Thomas   148 *Masham* (Rowe) Marsham   159 *Which I* (F2) which   176 *have sought* (Q) sought

II.3 3, 6 *earn* (Camb.) erne   16 *'a babbled* (Theobald) a Table   24 *upward and upward* (Q) vp-peer'd and vpward   47 *word* (Q) world

II.4 68 *followed* (Pope) followèd   79 *borrowed* (Pope) borrowèd   107 *privèd* (Walter) privy   109 *swallowed* (Pope) swallowèd   134 *difference* (Camb.) diff'rence

III.Cho. 4 *Hampton* (Theobald) Dover   6 *fanning* (Rowe) fayning   12 *furrowed* (Rowe) furrowèd

III.1 7 *summon* (Rowe) commune   17 *noble* (Malone) noblish   24 *men* (F4) me   32 *Straining* (Rowe) Straying

III.2 16 *hie* (Q) high   19 *preach* (Hanmer, as also for some similar normalizations of Welsh accent following) breach   62, 136–37 *petter* better   69, 80 *orld* world   70 *peard* beard   107 *trompet* trumpet   114 *ay'll lig* (Camb.) Ile ligge   115 *ay'll* (Camb.) Ile   128 *poth* both   129 *pirth* birth   138 *pold* bold

III.3 16 *Arrayed* (Pope) Arrayèd   32 *heady* (F2) headly   35 *Defile* (Rowe) Desire

III.4 2 *parles* (Warburton) parlas   4 *enseigner* (F2) ensigniez; *j'apprends* (this ed.) ie apprend   6, 17, 24 *est* (F2) &   7 *Et les doigts* (misplaced in a separate speech given to *Alice* in F; corrected by Theobald) *Et les* (Capell) E le   8 ALICE (Theobald) Kat; *Les* (Capell) Le; *les* (Capell) e   9 *souviendrai* (F2) souemeray   11 KATHERINE (Theobald) Alice (F, with

proper assignment to Katherine restored at *j'ai gagné*) *de fingres* (Capell)
le Fingres   **11, 13** *les* (Capell) le   **14** *Les* (F2) Le   **20** *Et le* (F2) E de
36 *la* (F2) de   **38** *N'avez-vous pas* (F2) N'ave vos y; *déjà* (Warburton)
desia   **40** *Non* (Warburton) Nome   **44** *Sauf* (Rowe) Sans   **45** *dis-je*
(F2) de ie   **46** *le* (Capell) les; *la* (Capell) de; *robe* (Rowe) roba   **47, 48**
De . . . de (Capell) Le . . . le   **50** *les* (F2) le   **51** *ces* (F2) ce; *les* (F2) le
52 *Foh!* (Camb.) fo; *de* (Capell) le   **53** *Néantmoins* (F2) neant moys
55 *de count* (Warburton) le count

III.5 7 *scions* (Var., 1803) Syens   **11** *de* (F2) du   **43** *Vaudemont* (F2) Van-
demont   **45** *Foix* (Capell) Loys   **46** *knights* (Theobald conj.; Pope)
Kings

III.6 4, 11 *pridge* Bridge   **10** *plessed* blessed   **10, 15, 82** *orld* world   **30,
31** *plind* blind   **30** *her* (Q) his   **53** *prother* Brother   **98** *Pardolph* Bardolph   **100** *plows* blows   **109** *lenity* (Q) Leuitie

III.7 12 *pasterns* (F2) postures; *Ça* (Theobald) ch'   **58** *lief* (Capell) liue
63–64 *vomissement* (F2) vemissement   **64** *et la truie* (Rowe) est la leuye

IV.Cho. 16 *name* (Tyrwhitt conj.; Steevens) nam'd   **20** *cripple* (Theobald)
creeple –   **27** *Presenteth* (Hanmer) Presented

IV.1 3 *Good* (F3) God   **63 s.d.** *The . . . aside* (this ed.) Manet King   **65**
Cheshu Jesu   **66** *orld* world   **71** *pabble* babble   **93** *Thomas* (Theobald)
John   **238** *What is* (Knight) What? is; *adoration* (F2) Odoration   **246**
Think'st (Rowe) Thinks   **268** *Hyperion* (F2) Hiperio   **284** *if* (Tyrwhitt
conj.; Steevens) of   **289** *bestowed* (Pope) bestowèd

IV.2 4 *eaux* (Theobald) ewes   **5** *les* (this ed.) le   **6** *Cieux* (Munro, as
"cieu") Cien   **11** *dout* (Rowe) doubt   **25** *'gainst* (F2) against   **49** *gimmaled* (Delius) Iymold

IV.3 6 *be wi'* (Gurr) bye (F)   **14–15** *And . . . valor* (after 1.11 in F; correction by Theobald supported by Q)   **49** *And . . . day* (Q) Omitted   **60**
rememberèd (Rowe) rememb'red   **100** *buried* (Eds.) buryèd

IV.4 12 *pitié* (F2) pitez   **15** *Or* (Hanmer) For   **35** *de* (F2) a *faites* (Malone) faite   **38** *cuppe le* (This ed.) cuppele   **40** *O'er* (This ed.) Or   **52**
néantmoins (F2) neant-mons   **54** *l'avez promis* (Malone) layt a promets
56 *remercîmens* (F2) remercious; *j'ai tombé* (This ed.) Je intombe   **58**
distingué (Capell) distinie   **66** *Suivez* (Rowe) Saaue

IV.5 2 *perdu . . . est perdu* (Rowe) perdia . . . et perdie   **3** *Mort de* (Rowe)
Mor Dieu   **12** *honor* (Q) Omitted   **16** *by a slave* (Q) a base slave   **24**
Exeunt (Eds.) Exit

IV.6 15 *And* (Q) He   **34** *my full* (Craik) mistful (Theobald) mixtful

IV.7 26, 31 *poth* both   **47** *pelly* belly   **77** *the* (Capell) with   **100** *padge*
badge   **110** *Chesu* Jeshu   **113** *God* (F3) Good   **123** *'a live* (Capell)
aliue   **138** *plack* blacke

IV.8 10, 43 *orld* world   **34** *peggarly* beggarly   **62** *pelly* belly   **65** *petter*
better   **97** *Foix* (Capell) Foyes   **111** *we* (F2) me

V.1 5 *peggarly* beggarly   **6** *orld* world   **9** *pid* bid   **10** *preed* breed   **11**
pold bold   **39** *Pite* Bite   **53** *proken* broken   **63** *be wi'* (Gurr) bye (F)
86 *swear* (F3) swore

V.2 12 *England* (F2) Ireland   **45** *fumitory* (F4) Femetary   **50** *all* (Rowe)
withall   **77** *cursitory* (Wilson) curselarie   **98 s.d.** (Gurr) omnes, manet.
(F)   **183** *est* (Pope) & *meilleur* (Hanmer) melius   **253** *abaissiez* (John-

son) abbaise *grandeur* (F2) grandeus **254** *de vostre* (Camb.) nostre *seigneurie* (Camb.) Seigneur **259** *coutume* (Rowe) costume **262** *baiser* (Hanmer) buisse **267** *vraiment* (Hanmer) verayment **320** *never* (Rowe) Omitted **336** *Héritier* (Rowe) Heretere **361** *paction* (Theobald) Pation

The Life of
King Henry the Fifth

[NAMES OF THE ACTORS

CHORUS
KING HENRY THE FIFTH
DUKES OF GLOUCESTER AND BEDFORD, *brothers to the king*
DUKE OF EXETER, *uncle to the king*
DUKE OF YORK, *cousin to the king*
EARLS OF SALISBURY, WESTMORELAND, WARWICK, AND CAMBRIDGE
ARCHBISHOP OF CANTERBURY
BISHOP OF ELY
LORD SCROOP
SIR THOMAS GREY
SIR THOMAS ERPINGHAM
GOWER, FLUELLEN, MACMORRIS, JAMY, *English officers*
JOHN BATES, ALEXANDER COURT, MICHAEL WILLIAMS, *English soldiers*
PISTOL, NYM, BARDOLPH
BOY
AN ENGLISH HERALD
CHARLES THE SIXTH, *King of France*
LEWIS, *the Dauphin*
DUKES OF BURGUNDY, ORLEANS, BOURBON, AND BRITAINE
THE CONSTABLE OF FRANCE
RAMBURES, GRANDPRÉ, *French lords*
GOVERNOR OF HARFLEUR
MONTJOY, *a French herald*
AMBASSADORS TO KING HENRY
ISABEL, *Queen of France*
KATHERINE, *daughter to the French king and queen*
ALICE, *an attendant to Katherine*
HOSTESS QUICKLY OF AN EASTCHEAP TAVERN, *wife to Pistol*
LORDS, LADIES, OFFICERS, SOLDIERS, CITIZENS, MESSENGERS, AND ATTENDANTS

SCENE: *England and France*]

✴

The Life of
King Henry the Fifth

⮑ *Enter Prologue.*

O for a Muse of fire, that would ascend 1
The brightest heaven of invention; 2
A kingdom for a stage, princes to act
And monarchs to behold the swelling scene! 4
Then should the warlike Harry, like himself, 5
Assume the port of Mars, and at his heels, 6
Leashed in like hounds, should famine, sword, and fire
Crouch for employment. But pardon, gentles all, 8
The flat unraisèd spirits that hath dared
On this unworthy scaffold to bring forth 10
So great an object. Can this cockpit hold 11
The vasty fields of France? Or may we cram 12
Within this wooden O the very casques 13
That did affright the air at Agincourt? 14
O, pardon! since a crooked figure may 15
Attest in little place a million; 16
And let us, ciphers to this great account, 17

Pro. **1** *fire* (most buoyant of the four elements: earth, water, air, fire; the one that ascended to the empyrean) **2** *invention* imagination **4** *swelling* increasing in grandeur **5** *like* in a manner worthy of **6** *port* bearing **8** *Crouch* i.e., kneel obsequiously; *gentles* nobles **10** *scaffold* stage **11** *cockpit* an arena for animal fighting **12** *vasty* vast **13** *wooden O* circular theater (such as the Globe); *the very casques* i.e., even the helmets **14** *Agincourt* battlefield in France **15** *crooked figure* cipher or zero (which appended to a number will multiply it tenfold) **16** *Attest . . . place* stand for **17** *account* (1) total, (2) story

On your imaginary forces work.
19 Suppose within the girdle of these walls
20 Are now confined two mighty monarchies,
21 Whose high-uprearèd and abutting fronts
22 The perilous narrow ocean parts asunder.
23 Piece out our imperfections with your thoughts:
Into a thousand parts divide one man
25 And make imaginary puissance.
Think, when we talk of horses, that you see them
Printing their proud hoofs i' th' receiving earth;
28 For 'tis your thoughts that now must deck our kings,
Carry them here and there, jumping o'er times,
30 Turning th' accomplishment of many years
31 Into an hourglass – for the which supply,
Admit me Chorus to this history,
Who, Prologue-like, your humble patience pray,
Gently to hear, kindly to judge, our play.   *Exit.*

*

∽ **I.1** *Enter the two Bishops, [the Archbishop] of
Canterbury and [the Bishop of] Ely.*

CANTERBURY
1 My lord, I'll tell you, that self bill is urged
Which in th' eleventh year of the last king's reign
3 Was like, and had indeed against us passed
4 But that the scambling and unquiet time
5 Did push it out of farther question.
ELY
But how, my lord, shall we resist it now?
CANTERBURY
It must be thought on. If it pass against us,

---

19 *girdle* encircling frame 21 *fronts* frontiers, foreheads 22 *narrow ocean*
i.e., the English Channel 23 *Piece out* supplement 25 *puissance* armed
forces 28 *deck* clothe 31 *hourglass* i.e., short measure of time; *for . . . supply* in aid whereof
   I.1 Within the palace of the King of England 1 *self* selfsame 3 *like*
likely 4 *scambling* unsettled 5 *question* discussion

We lose the better half of our possession;
For all the temporal lands which men devout   9
By testament have given to the Church   10
Would they strip from us; being valued thus –
As much as would maintain, to the king's honor,
Full fifteen earls and fifteen hundred knights,
Six thousand and two hundred good esquires,   14
And to relief of lazars, and weak age   15
Of indigent faint souls past corporal toil,
A hundred almshouses right well supplied;   17
And to the coffers of the king beside
A thousand pounds by th' year. Thus runs the bill.

ELY
This would drink deep.   20
CANTERBURY   'Twould drink the cup and all.
ELY
But what prevention?
CANTERBURY
The king is full of grace and fair regard.   22
ELY
And a true lover of the holy Church.
CANTERBURY
The courses of his youth promised it not.   24
The breath no sooner left his father's body
But that his wildness, mortified in him,   26
Seemed to die too. Yea, at that very moment
Consideration like an angel came   28
And whipped th' offending Adam out of him,
Leaving his body as a paradise   30
T' envelop and contain celestial spirits.
Never was such a sudden scholar made;
Never came reformation in a flood

---

9 *temporal* secular   10 *testament* will   14 *esquires* (a rank below knight)   15
lazars lepers   17 *almshouses* poorhouses   22 *fair regard* benign temper   24
courses phases (?)   26 *mortified* struck dead   28 *Consideration* penitent re-
flection

34 With such a heady currance scouring faults,
35 Nor never Hydra-headed willfulness
36 So soon did lose his seat – and all at once –
    As in this king.
    ELY   We are blessèd in the change.
    CANTERBURY
38 Hear him but reason in divinity,
    And, all-admiring, with an inward wish
40 You would desire the king were made a prelate;
    Hear him debate of commonwealth affairs,
    You would say it hath been all in all his study;
43 List his discourse of war, and you shall hear
    A fearful battle rendered you in music;
45 Turn him to any cause of policy,
46 The Gordian knot of it he will unloose,
47 Familiar as his garter; that when he speaks,
48 The air, a chartered libertine, is still,
49 And the mute wonder lurketh in men's ears
50 To steal his sweet and honeyed sentences;
51 So that the art and practic part of life
    Must be the mistress to this theoric;
53 Which is a wonder how his grace should glean it,
54 Since his addiction was to courses vain,
55 His companies unlettered, rude, and shallow,
    His hours filled up with riots, banquets, sports;
    And never noted in him any study,
    Any retirement, any sequestration
59 From open haunts and popularity.

---

34 *heady currance* headlong current   35 *Hydra* the monster with proliferating heads slain by Hercules   36 *his seat* its throne   38 *divinity* theology   40 *prelate* priest   43 *List* listen to   45 *cause of policy* political issue   46 *Gordian knot* intricate knot cut by Alexander in asserting his destiny to rule over Asia   47 *Familiar* offhandedly, mechanically; *garter* stocking fastener   48 *chartered* licensed; *libertine* one free from bondage or restraint   49 *the . . . ears* the wonder renders men silent in order to listen   51–52 *the art . . . theoric* i.e., study and practice must be the teacher of this mastery of theory   53 *glean* gather   54 *courses* pursuits   55 *unlettered* illiterate   59 *open haunts* places of public resort; *popularity* ordinary people

ELY
   The strawberry grows underneath the nettle,   60
   And wholesome berries thrive and ripen best
   Neighbored by fruit of baser quality;   62
   And so the prince obscured his contemplation   63
   Under the veil of wildness, which, no doubt,
   Grew like the summer grass, fastest by night,
   Unseen, yet crescive in his faculty.   66

CANTERBURY
   It must be so, for miracles are ceased
   And therefore we must needs admit the means   68
   How things are perfected.

ELY   But, my good lord,
   How now for mitigation of this bill   70
   Urged by the Commons? Doth his majesty   71
   Incline to it or no?

CANTERBURY   He seems indifferent,
   Or rather swaying more upon our part
   Than cherishing th' exhibiters against us;   74
   For I have made an offer to his majesty,
   Upon our spiritual Convocation   76
   And in regard of causes now in hand   77
   Which I have opened to his grace at large
   As touching France, to give a greater sum   79
   Than ever at one time the clergy yet   80
   Did to his predecessors part withal.

ELY
   How did this offer seem received, my lord?

CANTERBURY
   With good acceptance of his majesty,   83
   Save that there was not time enough to hear,
   As I perceived his grace would fain have done,   85

---

62 *baser* lower born **63** *obscured* hid **66** *crescive . . . faculty* i.e., given to growth **68** *means* i.e., natural means **71** *Commons* lower house of Parliament **74** *exhibiters* introducers of the bill **76** *Upon* on behalf of **77** *causes . . . hand* present concerns (i.e., the war in France) **79** *touching* concerning **83** *of* by **85** *fain* rather

86 The severals and unhidden passages
 Of his true titles to some certain dukedoms,
 And generally to the crown and seat of France
89 Derived from Edward his great-grandfather.

ELY

90 What was th' impediment that broke this off?

CANTERBURY
 The French ambassador upon that instant
 Craved audience; and the hour I think is come
 To give him hearing. Is it four o'clock?

ELY
 It is.

CANTERBURY
 Then go we in to know his embassy,
 Which I could with a ready guess declare
 Before the Frenchman speak a word of it.

ELY
 I'll wait upon you, and I long to hear it.   *Exeunt.*

*

❧ **I.2** *Enter the King, Humphrey [Duke of Gloucester],*
 Bedford, Clarence, Warwick, Westmoreland, and
 Exeter [with Attendants].

KING
 Where is my gracious Lord of Canterbury?

EXETER

2 Not here in presence.

KING   Send for him, good uncle.

WESTMORELAND

3 Shall we call in th' ambassador, my liege?

KING

4 Not yet, my cousin. We would be resolved,

---

86 *severals* particulars; *unhidden passages* clear claims 89 *Edward* i.e., King
Edward III
 I.2 The presence chamber of the palace **s.d.** *Clarence* (a "ghost" character, appearing only in this single stage direction) 2 *presence* royal presence;
state 3 *liege* lord 4 *We* (the royal pronoun); *resolved* freed from doubt

Before we hear him, of some things of weight   5
That task our thoughts concerning us and France.   6
   Enter two Bishops [the Archbishop of Canterbury and
   the Bishop of Ely].

CANTERBURY
God and his angels guard your sacred throne
And make you long become it!

KING   Sure we thank you.
My learnèd lord, we pray you to proceed
And justly and religiously unfold   10
Why the Law Salic, that they have in France,   11
Or should or should not bar us in our claim.   12
And God forbid, my dear and faithful lord,
That you should fashion, wrest, or bow your reading,
Or nicely charge your understanding soul   15
With opening titles miscreate, whose right   16
Suits not in native colors with the truth;
For God doth know how many now in health
Shall drop their blood in approbation   19
Of what your reverence shall incite us to.   20
Therefore take heed how you impawn our person,   21
How you awake our sleeping sword of war.
We charge you in the name of God take heed;
For never two such kingdoms did contend
Without much fall of blood, whose guiltless drops
Are every one a woe, a sore complaint   26
'Gainst him whose wrongs gives edge unto the swords   27
That makes such waste in brief mortality.
Under this conjuration speak, my lord;
For we will hear, note, and believe in heart   30
That what you speak is in your conscience washed
As pure as sin with baptism.   32

─────────

5 *of weight* serious   6 *task* burden   11 *Law Salic* the law that forbids inheri-
tance through the female line   12 *Or* either; *claim* i.e., to the French throne
15 *nicely charge* rationalize   16–17 *opening . . . colors* advancing illegitimate
claims, the validity of which fails to harmonize   19 *approbation* support
21 *impawn* engage   26 *woe* grievance   27 *wrongs* wrongdoing   32 *sin* original sin

CANTERBURY

33   Then hear me, gracious sovereign, and you peers,
    That owe yourselves, your lives, and services
35   To this imperial throne. There is no bar
    To make against your highness' claim to France
37   But this which they produce from Pharamond:
    "In terram Salicam mulieres ne succedant";
    "No woman shall succeed in Salic land."
40   Which Salic land the French unjustly gloze
    To be the realm of France, and Pharamond
    The founder of this law and female bar.
    Yet their own authors faithfully affirm
    That the land Salic is in Germany,
45   Between the floods of Sala and of Elbe;
46   Where Charles the Great, having subdued the Saxons,
    There left behind and settled certain French;
    Who, holding in disdain the German women
49   For some dishonest manners of their life,
50   Established then this law: to wit, no female
    Should be inheritrix in Salic land;
    Which Salic, as I said, 'twixt Elbe and Sala
    Is at this day in Germany called Meisen.
    Then doth it well appear the Salic Law
    Was not devisèd for the realm of France;
    Nor did the French possess the Salic land
    Until four hundred one and twenty years
58   After defunction of King Pharamond,
    Idly supposed the founder of this law,
60   Who died within the year of our redemption
    Four hundred twenty-six; and Charles the Great
    Subdued the Saxons, and did seat the French
    Beyond the river Sala, in the year
    Eight hundred five. Besides, their writers say,
    King Pepin, which deposèd Childeric,

---

33 *peers* lords   35 *bar* obstacle   37 *they* the French; *Pharamond* legendary
Frankish king   40 *gloze* interpret   45 *floods* rivers   46 *Charles the Great*
Charlemagne   49 *dishonest* unchaste   58 *defunction* death

Did, as heir general, being descended
Of Blithild, which was daughter to King Clothair,
Make claim and title to the crown of France.
Hugh Capet also, who usurped the crown
Of Charles the Duke of Lorraine, sole heir male   70
Of the true line and stock of Charles the Great,
To find his title with some shows of truth,   72
Though in pure truth it was corrupt and naught,
Conveyed himself as th' heir to th' Lady Lingard,
Daughter to Charlemain, who was the son   75
To Lewis the Emperor, and Lewis the son
Of Charles the Great. Also King Lewis the Tenth,   77
Who was sole heir to the usurper Capet,
Could not keep quiet in his conscience,
Wearing the crown of France, till satisfied   80
That fair Queen Isabel, his grandmother,
Was lineal of the Lady Ermengard,   82
Daughter to Charles the foresaid Duke of Lorraine;
By the which marriage the line of Charles the Great
Was reunited to the crown of France.
So that, as clear as is the summer's sun,
King Pepin's title and Hugh Capet's claim,
King Lewis his satisfaction, all appear   88
To hold in right and title of the female:
So do the kings of France unto this day,   90
Howbeit they would hold up this Salic Law   91
To bar your highness claiming from the female,
And rather choose to hide them in a net   93
Than amply to imbar their crooked titles   94
Usurped from you and your progenitors.

KING
    May I with right and conscience make this claim?

---

72 *find* furnish; *shows* appearances   75, 77 *Charlemain, Lewis the Tenth* (ac-
tually Charles the Bald and Louis IX; errors repeated from the chronicles of
Hall and Holinshed)   82 *lineal* descended lineally   88 *his satisfaction* i.e.,
King Lewis's conviction   91 *Howbeit* howsoever   93 *hide . . . net* cover
themselves in a web of contradictions   94 *imbar* bar claim to, impeach;
crooked ill-gotten

CANTERBURY
    The sin upon my head, dread sovereign!
98 For in the Book of Numbers is it writ:
    When the man dies, let the inheritance
100 Descend unto the daughter. Gracious lord,
101 Stand for your own, unwind your bloody flag,
    Look back into your mighty ancestors;
    Go, my dread lord, to your great-grandsire's tomb,
    From whom you claim; invoke his warlike spirit,
    And your great-uncle's, Edward the Black Prince,
106 Who on the French ground played a tragedy,
107 Making defeat on the full power of France,
    Whiles his most mighty father on a hill
    Stood smiling to behold his lion's whelp
110 Forage in blood of French nobility.
111 O noble English, that could entertain
    With half their forces the full pride of France
    And let another half stand laughing by,
114 All out of work and cold for action!
        ELY
    Awake remembrance of these valiant dead,
116 And with your puissant arm renew their feats.
    You are their heir; you sit upon their throne;
118 The blood and courage that renownèd them
    Runs in your veins; and my thrice-puissant liege
120 Is in the very May-morn of his youth,
    Ripe for exploits and mighty enterprises.
        EXETER
    Your brother kings and monarchs of the earth
    Do all expect that you should rouse yourself
    As did the former lions of your blood.
        WESTMORELAND
    They know your grace hath cause, and means, and
        might —

---

98 *Numbers* (see Numbers 27 : 8) **101** *own* i.e., own claim **106** *tragedy*
i.e., Battle of Crécy, 1346 **107** *on* of **110** *Forage in* prey on **111** *entertain*
engage **114** *cold for action* stiff on account of inaction **116** *puissant* powerful **118** *renownèd* brought renown to

So hath your highness! Never king of England   126
  Had nobles richer and more loyal subjects,
  Whose hearts have left their bodies here in England
  And lie pavilioned in the fields of France.   129

CANTERBURY
  O, let their bodies follow, my dear liege,   *130*
  With blood, and sword, and fire to win your right!
  In aid whereof we of the spiritualty   132
  Will raise your highness such a mighty sum
  As never did the clergy at one time
  Bring in to any of your ancestors.

KING
  We must not only arm t' invade the French,
  But lay down our proportions to defend   137
  Against the Scot, who will make road upon us   138
  With all advantages.   139

CANTERBURY
  They of those marches, gracious sovereign,   140
  Shall be a wall sufficient to defend
  Our inland from the pilfering borderers.   142

KING
  We do not mean the coursing snatchers only,   143
  But fear the main intendment of the Scot,
  Who hath been still a giddy neighbor to us;   145
  For you shall read that my great-grandfather
  Never went with his forces into France
  But that the Scot on his unfurnished kingdom   148
  Came pouring like the tide into a breach,
  With ample and brim fullness of his force,   *150*
  Galling the gleanèd land with hot assays,   151

---

126 *So* so indeed   129 *pavilioned* in tents of war   132 *spiritualty* clergy
137 *lay . . . proportions* estimate our forces   138 *road* inroads   139 *all advantages* every opportunity   140 *marches* i.e., northern borderlands   142
Our inland our country's interior areas; *borderers* those living on the border
of England and Scotland   143 *coursing snatchers* mounted raiders   145 *still*
always; *giddy* unstable   148 *unfurnished* unprepared   151 *Galling* bruising;
gleanèd stripped (of manpower); *assays* attempts

152   Girding with grievous siege castles and towns;
        That England, being empty of defense,
154   Hath shook and trembled at th' ill neighborhood.

CANTERBURY

155   She hath been then more feared than harmed, my liege;
156   For hear her but exampled by herself;
        When all her chivalry hath been in France
        And she a mourning widow of her nobles,
        She hath herself not only well defended
160   But taken and impounded as a stray
        The King of Scots; whom she did send to France
162   To fill King Edward's fame with prisoner kings,
163   And make her chronicle as rich with praise
164   As is the ooze and bottom of the sea
165   With sunken wrack and sumless treasuries.

ELY

        But there's a saying very old and true:
            "If that you will France win,
              Then with Scotland first begin."
169   For once the eagle England being in prey,
170   To her unguarded nest the weasel Scot
        Comes sneaking, and so sucks her princely eggs,
        Playing the mouse in absence of the cat,
173   To 'tame and havoc more than she can eat.

EXETER

        It follows then, the cat must stay at home;
175   Yet that is but a crushed necessity,
176   Since we have locks to safeguard necessaries
177   And pretty traps to catch the petty thieves.
        While that the armèd hand doth fight abroad,
179   Th' advisèd head defends itself at home;

---

152 *Girding* encircling   154 *neighborhood* neighborliness   155 *feared* frightened   156 *exampled* represented (by an incident in the past)   160 *as a stray* like a stray beast   162 *fill* increase   163 *chronicle* historical account 164 *ooze and bottom* oozy bottom   165 *sumless* inestimable   169 *being in prey* having become a predator   173 *'tame* attame, broach   175 *crushed necessity* voided conclusion   176 *necessaries* essentials   177 *pretty* neat   179 *advisèd* prudent

For government, though high, and low, and lower,   180
Put into parts, doth keep in one consent,   181
Congreeing in a full and natural close   182
Like the music.
CANTERBURY   Therefore doth heaven divide
The state of man in divers functions,   184
Setting endeavor in continual motion;
To which is fixèd as an aim or butt   186
Obedience; for so work the honeybees,
Creatures that by a rule in nature teach
The act of order to a peopled kingdom.
They have a king, and officers of sorts,   190
Where some like magistrates correct at home,   191
Others like merchants venture trade abroad,
Others like soldiers armèd in their stings
Make boot upon the summer's velvet buds,   194
Which pillage they with merry march bring home   195
To the tent royal of their emperor,
Who, busied in his majesties, surveys   197
The singing masons building roofs of gold,
The civil citizens kneading up the honey,
The poor mechanic porters crowding in   200
Their heavy burdens at his narrow gate,
The sad-eyed justice with his surly hum   202
Delivering o'er to executors pale   203
The lazy yawning drone. I this infer,
That many things having full reference   205
To one consent may work contrariously,   206
As many arrows loosèd several ways   207

180–81 *though . . . parts* i.e., though made up of three estates   181 *Put into parts* divided into separate functions or ranks; *one* mutual; *consent* intention   182 *Congreeing* agreeing; *close* cadence   184 *divers* several   186 *fixèd as* attached like; *aim or butt* i.e., target   190 *king* (the queen bee was mistaken for male until the late seventeenth century)   191 *correct* rule   194 *Make boot* prey   195 *pillage* booty   197 *majesties* royal functions   200 *mechanic* artisan   202 *sad-eyed* solemn-eyed   203 *executors* executioners   205–6 *reference . . . consent* i.e., relationship to a single agreement   206 *contrariously* diversely   207 *loosèd . . . ways* i.e., shot from different angles

Come to one mark;
As many several ways meet in one town,
210 As many fresh streams meet in one salt sea,
211 As many lines close in the dial's center;
So may a thousand actions, once afoot,
End in one purpose, and be all well borne
Without defeat. Therefore to France, my liege!
Divide your happy England into four,
Whereof take you one quarter into France,
217 And you withal shall make all Gallia shake.
If we, with thrice such powers left at home,
Cannot defend our own doors from the dog,
220 Let us be worried, and our nation lose
221 The name of hardiness and policy.

KING

222 Call in the messengers sent from the Dauphin.
                    [Exeunt some Attendants.]
Now are we well resolved, and by God's help
224 And yours, the noble sinews of our power,
225 France being ours, we'll bend it to our awe
Or break it all to pieces. Or there we'll sit,
227 Ruling in large and ample empery
O'er France and all her almost kingly dukedoms,
229 Or lay these bones in an unworthy urn,
230 Tombless, with no remembrance over them.
Either our history shall with full mouth
Speak freely of our acts, or else our grave,
Like Turkish mute, shall have a tongueless mouth,
234 Not worshiped with a waxen epitaph.
        Enter Ambassadors of France [attended].
Now are we well prepared to know the pleasure
Of our fair cousin Dauphin; for we hear
Your greeting is from him, not from the king.

---

211 *dial's* i.e., of a sundial   217 *Gallia* France   221 *policy* statesmanship
222 *Dauphin* French prince and heir apparent   224 *yours* i.e., his nobles'
225 *our awe* awe of us   227 *empery* sovereignty   229 *these* i.e., his own
234 *with . . . epitaph* i.e., with even so much as a wax (as opposed to durable
bronze) epitaph

AMBASSADOR
    May't please your majesty to give us leave
    Freely to render what we have in charge,
    Or shall we sparingly show you far off   240
    The Dauphin's meaning and our embassy?
KING
    We are no tyrant, but a Christian king,
    Unto whose grace our passion is as subject   243
    As is our wretches fettered in our prisons.
    Therefore with frank and with uncurbèd plainness
    Tell us the Dauphin's mind.
AMBASSADOR   Thus then, in few:
    Your highness, lately sending into France,
    Did claim some certain dukedoms in the right
    Of your great predecessor, King Edward the Third.
    In answer of which claim, the prince our master   250
    Says that you savor too much of your youth,   251
    And bids you be advised: There's naught in France   252
    That can be with a nimble galliard won;   253
    You cannot revel into dukedoms there.
    He therefore sends you, meeter for your spirit,   255
    This tun of treasure; and in lieu of this,   256
    Desires you let the dukedoms that you claim
    Hear no more of you. This the Dauphin speaks.
KING
    What treasure, uncle?
EXETER   Tennis balls, my liege.
KING
    We are glad the Dauphin is so pleasant with us.   260
    His present and your pains we thank you for.
    When we have matched our rackets to these balls,
    We will in France, by God's grace, play a set
    Shall strike his father's crown into the hazard.   264

---

243 *passion* i.e., temper   **251** *savor* taste   **252** *be advised* take counsel   **253**
galliard merry dance   **255** *meeter* more appropriate   **256** *tun* box, casket
264 *crown* (1) symbol of majesty, (2) wager money; *hazard* (1) a goal in an
Elizabethan tennis court, (2) jeopardy

265   Tell him he hath made a match with such a wrangler
266   That all the courts of France will be disturbed
267   With chases. And we understand him well,
268   How he comes o'er us with our wilder days,
        Not measuring what use we made of them.
270   We never valued this poor seat of England,
271   And therefore, living hence, did give ourself
        To barbarous license; as 'tis ever common
        That men are merriest when they are from home.
274   But tell the Dauphin I will keep my state,
        Be like a king, and show my sail of greatness
276   When I do rouse me in my throne of France.
277   For that I have laid by my majesty
        And plodded like a man for working days,
        But I will rise there with so full a glory
280   That I will dazzle all the eyes of France,
        Yea, strike the Dauphin blind to look on us.
        And tell the pleasant prince this mock of his
283   Hath turned his balls to gunstones, and his soul
284   Shall stand sore chargèd for the wasteful vengeance
        That shall fly with them; for many a thousand widows
        Shall this his mock mock out of their dear husbands,
        Mock mothers from their sons, mock castles down;
288   And some are yet ungotten and unborn
        That shall have cause to curse the Dauphin's scorn.
290   But this lies all within the will of God,
        To whom I do appeal, and in whose name,
        Tell you the Dauphin, I am coming on
293   To venge me as I may, and to put forth
        My rightful hand in a well-hallowed cause.
        So get you hence in peace. And tell the Dauphin
        His jest will savor but of shallow wit

---

265 *wrangler* opponent   266 *courts* (1) tennis courts, (2) royal courts   267
chases (1) unsuccessful attempts to return tennis ball on first bounce, (2) pursuits   268 *comes o'er* taunts   271 *hence* i.e., out of our proper realm (France)
274 *state* kingly decorum   276 *rouse me in* mount   277 *For that* on account
of   283 *gunstones* cannonballs   284 *sore chargèd* grievously accused   288
ungotten unconceived   293 *venge me* avenge myself

When thousands weep more than did laugh at it.
Convey them with safe conduct. Fare you well.

Exeunt Ambassadors.

EXETER

This was a merry message.

KING

We hope to make the sender blush at it.   300
Therefore, my lords, omit no happy hour
That may give furth'rance to our expedition;
For we have now no thought in us but France,
Save those to God, that run before our business.
Therefore let our proportions for these wars   305
Be soon collected, and all things thought upon
That may with reasonable swiftness add
More feathers to our wings; for, God before,   308
We'll chide this Dauphin at his father's door.
Therefore let every man now task his thought   310
That this fair action may on foot be brought. *Exeunt.*

*

◈ **II.Cho.** *Flourish. Enter Chorus.*

Now all the youth of England are on fire,
And silken dalliance in the wardrobe lies.   2
Now thrive the armorers, and honor's thought   3
Reigns solely in the breast of every man.
They sell the pasture now to buy the horse,
Following the mirror of all Christian kings   6
With wingèd heels, as English Mercuries.   7
For now sits Expectation in the air
And hides a sword, from hilts unto the point,   9
With crowns imperial, crowns, and coronets   10

---

305 *proportions* required forces   308 *God before* i.e., God leading   310 *task*
exert
　　II.Cho.   2 *silken dalliance* pleasure garments of silk   3 *armorers* makers
of armor   6 *mirror* image, pattern   7 *Mercuries* (Mercury, messenger of the
gods, was usually pictured wearing winged sandals)   9 *hides a sword* i.e.,
completely impaled with captured crowns

Promised to Harry and his followers.
The French, advised by good intelligence
Of this most dreadful preparation,
14 Shake in their fear, and with pale policy
Seek to divert the English purposes.
16 O England! model to thy inward greatness,
Like little body with a mighty heart,
What mightst thou do that honor would thee do,
19 Were all thy children kind and natural!
20 But see, thy fault France hath in thee found out,
21 A nest of hollow bosoms, which he fills
22 With treacherous crowns; and three corrupted men –
One, Richard Earl of Cambridge, and the second,
Henry Lord Scroop of Masham, and the third,
Sir Thomas Grey, knight, of Northumberland –
26 Have, for the gilt of France (O guilt indeed!),
Confirmed conspiracy with fearful France,
And by their hands this grace of kings must die,
If hell and treason hold their promises,
30 Ere he take ship for France, and in Southampton.
31 Linger your patience on, and we'll digest
Th' abuse of distance, force a play.
The sum is paid, the traitors are agreed,
The king is set from London, and the scene
Is now transported, gentles, to Southampton.
There is the playhouse now, there must you sit,
And thence to France shall we convey you safe
And bring you back, charming the narrow seas
39 To give you gentle pass; for, if we may,
40 We'll not offend one stomach with our play.

---

14 *pale policy* timorous intrigue   16 *model to* i.e., small visible replica of   19
kind loyal to kindred   21 *hollow bosoms* (1) hypocrites, (2) empty receptacles
for money   22 *crowns* (1) coins, (2) foreign powers   26 *gilt* i.e., gold crowns
31–32 *digest . . . play* shape events into dramatic form   39 *pass* passage   40
offend . . . stomach (1) make seasick, (2) displease

But, till the king come forth, and not till then,   41
Unto Southampton do we shift our scene.   *Exit.*

*

∾ **II.1** *Enter Corporal Nym and Lieutenant Bardolph.*

BARDOLPH   Well met, Corporal Nym.

NYM   Good morrow, Lieutenant Bardolph.

BARDOLPH   What, are Ancient Pistol and you friends yet?   3

NYM   For my part, I care not. I say little; but when time
shall serve, there shall be smiles – but that shall be as it
may. I dare not fight, but I will wink and hold out mine
iron. It is a simple one, but what though? It will toast   7
cheese, and it will endure cold as another man's sword
will – and there's an end.

BARDOLPH   I will bestow a breakfast to make you friends,   10
and we'll be all three sworn brothers to France. Let 't be
so, good Corporal Nym.

NYM   Faith, I will live so long as I may, that's the certain
of it; and when I cannot live any longer, I will do as I
may. That is my rest, that is the rendezvous of it.   15

BARDOLPH   It is certain, corporal, that he is married to
Nell Quickly, and certainly she did you wrong, for you
were trothplight to her.   18

NYM   I cannot tell. Things must be as they may. Men
may sleep, and they may have their throats about them   20
at that time, and some say knives have edges. It must be
as it may. Though patience be a tired mare, yet she will
plod. There must be conclusions. Well, I cannot tell.   23

Enter Pistol and [Hostess] Quickly.

BARDOLPH   Here comes Ancient Pistol and his wife.
Good corporal, be patient here.

---

41 *But, till* i.e., only when (ll. 41–42 were apparently added to the original
speech – cf. ll. 33–34 – when the following comic episode, still set in London, was interpolated)

  II.1 A London street   3 *Ancient* ensign, standard-bearer   7 *iron* sword
10 *bestow* i.e., as a gift   15 *rest* last stake (in the game of primero); *rendezvous*
resort   18 *trothplight* betrothed   23 *conclusions* i.e., an end to everything

26 NYM   How now, mine host Pistol?

PISTOL

27   Base tyke, call'st thou me host?
     Now by this hand I swear I scorn the term;
     Nor shall my Nell keep lodgers!

30 HOSTESS   No, by my troth, not long; for we cannot lodge
     and board a dozen or fourteen gentlewomen that live
     honestly by the prick of their needles but it will be
33   thought we keep a bawdy house straight. *[Nym and Pis-*
34   *tol draw.]* O well-a-day, Lady, if he be not hewn now,
35   we shall see willful adultery and murder committed.

36 BARDOLPH   Good   lieutenant – good   corporal – offer
     nothing here.

NYM   Pish!

39 PISTOL   Pish for thee, Iceland dog, thou prick-eared cur
40   of Iceland!

HOSTESS   Good Corporal Nym, show thy valor, and put
     up your sword.

43 NYM   Will you shog off? I would have you solus.

PISTOL

     "Solus," egregious dog? O viper vile!
45   The "solus" in thy most mervailous face!
     The "solus" in thy teeth, and in thy throat,
47   And in thy hateful lungs, yea, in thy maw, perdy!
48   And, which is worse, within thy nasty mouth!
     I do retort the "solus" in thy bowels;
50   For I can take, and Pistol's cock is up.
     And flashing fire will follow.

52 NYM   I am not Barbason; you cannot conjure me. I have
     an humor to knock you indifferently well. If you grow

---

26 *host* i.e., husband of Hostess Quickly   27 *tyke* cur   30 *troth* truth   33
bawdy house brothel   34 *if . . . hewn* i.e., if Nym is not cut down (?)   35
adultery (malapropism, for "battery"?)   36–37 *offer nothing* i.e., do not offer
to fight   39 *Iceland dog* (a breed with long hair and pointed ears)   43 *shog
off* move along; *solus* alone (taken by Pistol as an insult)   45 *mervailous* marvelous   47 *maw* belly; *perdy* (mild oath, from *"par dieu"*)   48 *nasty* foul-
speaking   50 *take* strike; *cock is up* i.e., anger is aroused (with play on
"cocked Pistol")   52 *Barbason* a devil

foul with me, Pistol, I will scour you with my rapier, as   54
I may, in fair terms. If you would walk off, I would
prick your guts a little in good terms, as I may, and
that's the humor of it.

PISTOL

O braggart vile, and damnèd furious wight,   58
The grave doth gape, and doting death is near.
Therefore exhale!   60

BARDOLPH   Hear me, hear me what I say! He that strikes
the first stroke, I'll run him up to the hilts, as I am a
soldier.   *[Draws.]*

PISTOL

An oath of mickle might, and fury shall abate.   64
    [Pistol and Nym sheathe their swords.]
Give me thy fist, thy forefoot to me give.
Thy spirits are most tall.   66

NYM   I will cut thy throat one time or other in fair terms.
That is the humor of it.

PISTOL

Coupe la gorge!   69
That is the word. I thee defy again.   70
O hound of Crete, think'st thou my spouse to get?   71
No; to the spital go,   72
And from the powdering tub of infamy   73
Fetch forth the lazar kite of Cressid's kind,   74
Doll Tearsheet, she by name, and her espouse.   75
I have, and I will hold, the quondam Quickly   76
For the only she; and, pauca! there's enough.   77
Go to!
    Enter the Boy.

---

54 *foul* (from being fired);   *rapier* (serving as a scouring rod)   58 *wight* man
60 *exhale* draw (your sword)   64 *mickle* great   66 *tall* valiant   69 *Coupe la
gorge* cut the throat   71 *hound of Crete* (a shaggy breed)   72 *spital* hospital
73 *powdering tub* sweating tub (used as cure for venereal disease)   74 *lazar
kite* leprous bird of prey; *Cressid's kind* i.e., prostitute (this slang usage derives
from some versions of the Cressida story)   75 *her espouse* marry her   76
quondam former   77 *pauca* i.e., in few words

79 BOY   Mine host Pistol, you must come to my master –
80   and you, hostess. He is very sick and would to bed.
81   Good Bardolph, put thy face between his sheets and do
    the office of a warming pan. Faith, he's very ill.

BARDOLPH   Away, you rogue!

84 HOSTESS   By my troth, he'll yield the crow a pudding
85   one of these days. The king has killed his heart. Good
86   husband, come home presently.   *Exit.*

BARDOLPH   Come, shall I make you two friends? We
    must to France together: why the devil should we keep
    knives to cut one another's throats?

PISTOL
90   Let floods o'erswell and fiends for food howl on!

NYM   You'll pay me the eight shillings I won of you at
    betting?

PISTOL
    Base is the slave that pays.

NYM   That now I will have. That's the humor of it.

PISTOL
95   As manhood shall compound. Push home.
        [They] draw.

BARDOLPH   By this sword, he that makes the first thrust,
    I'll kill him! By this sword, I will.
        [Draws.]

PISTOL
98   "Sword" is an oath, and oaths must have their course.
        [Sheathes his sword.]

BARDOLPH   Corporal Nym, an thou wilt be friends, be
100   friends; an thou wilt not, why then be enemies with me
    too. Prithee put up.

PISTOL
102   A noble shalt thou have, and present pay;
    And liquor likewise will I give to thee

---

79 *master* i.e., Falstaff   81 *thy face* enflamed (with drink)   84 *yield . . . pudding* be executed and become food for crows   85 *his* i.e., Falstaff's, who was cast off by Prince Hal in *2 Henry IV*   86 *presently* at once   95 *compound* settle it   98 *Sword* i.e., S'word, or God's word   102 *noble* 6s. 8d.; *present pay* in cash

And friendship shall combine, and brotherhood.
I'll live by Nym, and Nym shall live by me.
Is not this just? For I shall sutler be   106
Unto the camp, and profits will accrue.
Give me thy hand.
      [Nym sheathes his sword.]
NYM   I shall have my noble?
PISTOL
In cash, most justly paid.   110
NYM   Well then, that's the humor of't.
      Enter Hostess.

HOSTESS   As ever you come of women, come in quickly   112
to Sir John. Ah, poor heart! he is so shaked of a burning
quotidian tertian that it is most lamentable to behold.   114
Sweet men, come to him.
NYM   The king hath run bad humors on the knight;
that's the even of it.   117
PISTOL
Nym, thou hast spoke the right.
His heart is fracted and corroborate.   119
NYM   The king is a good king, but it must be as it may: 120
he passes some humors and careers.   121
PISTOL
Let us condole the knight; for, lambkins, we will live.
                                                       [Exeunt.]

                              *

∾ **II.2** *Enter Exeter, Bedford, and Westmoreland.*

BEDFORD
'Fore God, his grace is bold to trust these traitors.

---

106 *sutler* vendor of liquor and provisions to an army   112 *come* are born
114 *quotidian tertian* (confusion of "tertian" fever, which occurs on alternate
days, with "quotidian," which occurs daily)   117 *the even of it* the long and
short of it, the plain truth   119 *fracted* broken; *corroborate* strengthened
121 *passes* lets pass by; *careers* capers
   II.2 The king's quarters at Southampton

EXETER
They shall be apprehended by and by.
WESTMORELAND
How smooth and even they do bear themselves,
As if allegiance in their bosoms sat
Crownèd with faith and constant loyalty!
BEDFORD
The king hath note of all that they intend
By interception which they dream not of.
EXETER

8   Nay, but the man that was his bedfellow,
9   Whom he hath dulled and cloyed with gracious favors –
10   That he should, for a foreign purse, so sell
His sovereign's life to death and treachery!
> *Sound trumpets. Enter the King, Scroop, Cambridge,*
> *and Grey [, Lords, and Attendants].*

KING
Now sits the wind fair, and we will aboard.
My Lord of Cambridge, and my kind Lord of Masham,
And you, my gentle knight, give me your thoughts.
Think you not that the powers we bear with us
Will cut their passage through the force of France,
Doing the execution and the act
18   For which we have in head assembled them?
SCROOP
No doubt, my liege, if each man do his best.
KING
20   I doubt not that, since we are well persuaded
We carry not a heart with us from hence
That grows not in a fair consent with ours,
Nor leave not one behind that doth not wish
Success and conquest to attend on us.
CAMBRIDGE
Never was monarch better feared and loved
Than is your majesty. There's not, I think, a subject

---

8 *bedfellow* favorite (perhaps Scroop: see ll. 94–99) 9 *dulled* worn out;
cloyed surfeited 18 *head* an army

That sits in heart-grief and uneasiness
Under the sweet shade of your government.

GREY
True. Those that were your father's enemies
Have steeped their galls in honey and do serve you   30
With hearts create of duty and of zeal.

KING
We therefore have great cause of thankfulness,
And shall forget the office of our hand   33
Sooner than quittance of desert and merit   34
According to the weight and worthiness.

SCROOP
So service shall with steelèd sinews toil,
And labor shall refresh itself with hope,
To do your grace incessant services.

KING
We judge no less. Uncle of Exeter,
Enlarge the man committed yesterday   40
That railed against our person. We consider   41
It was excess of wine that set him on,
And on his more advice, we pardon him.   43

SCROOP
That's mercy, but too much security: 44
Let him be punished, sovereign, lest example
Breed by his sufferance more of such a kind.   46

KING
O, let us yet be merciful.

CAMBRIDGE
So may your highness, and yet punish too.

GREY
Sir,
You show great mercy if you give him life   50
After the taste of much correction.

---

30 *galls* grievances   **33** *office* use   **34** *quittance* requital   **40** *Enlarge* set free
41 *railed* spoke rudely   **43** *more advice* i.e., recovered judgment   **44** *security*
overconfidence   **46** *his sufferance* toleration of him

KING
  Alas, your too much love and care of me
53 Are heavy orisons 'gainst this poor wretch.
54 If little faults proceeding on distemper
  Shall not be winked at, how shall we stretch our eye
56 When capital crimes, chewed, swallowed, and digested,
  Appear before us? We'll yet enlarge that man,
  Though Cambridge, Scroop, and Grey, in their dear care
  And tender preservation of our person,
60 Would have him punished. And now to our French
  causes.
61 Who are the late commissioners?
CAMBRIDGE
  I one, my lord.
63 Your highness bade me ask for it today.
SCROOP
  So did you me, my liege.
GREY
  And I, my royal sovereign.
KING
  Then, Richard Earl of Cambridge, there is yours;
  There yours, Lord Scroop of Masham; and, sir knight,
  Grey of Northumberland, this same is yours.
  Read them, and know I know your worthiness.
70 My Lord of Westmoreland, and uncle Exeter,
  We will aboard tonight. – Why, how now, gentlemen?
72 What see you in those papers that you lose
  So much complexion? – Look ye, how they change!
  Their cheeks are paper. – Why, what read you there
75 That hath so cowarded and chased your blood
76 Out of appearance?
CAMBRIDGE   I do confess my fault,
  And do submit me to your highness' mercy.

_____

53 *orisons* pleas, prayers   54 *proceeding on distemper* following drunkenness
56 *chewed . . . digested* i.e., premeditated   61 *late* recently appointed; *commissioners* regents to govern England in Henry's absence   63 *it* the commis-
sion   72–73 *lose . . . complexion* grow so pale   75 *cowarded* frightened   76
appearance sight

GREY, SCROOP
  To which we all appeal.

KING
  The mercy that was quick in us but late,   79
  By your own counsel is suppressed and killed.   80
  You must not dare for shame to talk of mercy;
  For your own reasons turn into your bosoms   82
  As dogs upon their masters, worrying you.
  See you, my princes and my noble peers,
  These English monsters! My Lord of Cambridge here – 85
  You know how apt our love was to accord   86
  To furnish him with all appurtenants
  Belonging to his honor; and this man
  Hath, for a few light crowns, lightly conspired
  And sworn unto the practices of France   90
  To kill us here in Hampton; to the which
  This knight, no less for bounty bound to us   92
  Than Cambridge is, hath likewise sworn. But O,
  What shall I say to thee, Lord Scroop, thou cruel,
  Ingrateful, savage, and inhuman creature?
  Thou that didst bear the key of all my counsels,
  That knew'st the very bottom of my soul,
  That almost mightst have coined me into gold,   98
  Wouldst thou have practiced on me for thy use?   99
  May it be possible that foreign hire   *100*
  Could out of thee extract one spark of evil
  That might annoy my finger? 'Tis so strange   102
  That, though the truth of it stands off as gross   103
  As black and white, my eye will scarcely see it.
  Treason and murder ever kept together,
  As two yoke-devils sworn to either's purpose,

---

79 *quick* living 82 *turn* return 85 *English* i.e., as opposed to foreign-born
(and hence more likely to be monstrous) 86 *accord* consent 90 *practices*
plots 92 *This knight* i.e., Grey 98 *coined . . . gold* i.e., in receiving money
from him 99 *use* (with wordplay on "interest income" – the historical
Scroop had been Lord Treasurer) 102 *annoy* injure 103 *gross* clearly

107 Working so grossly in a natural cause
    That admiration did not whoop at them;
109 But thou, 'gainst all proportion, didst bring in
110 Wonder to wait on treason and on murder;
    And whatsoever cunning fiend it was
112 That wrought upon thee so preposterously
113 Hath got the voice in hell for excellence.
114 All other devils that suggest by treasons
115 Do botch and bungle up damnation
    With patches, colors, and with forms being fetched
    From glist'ring semblances of piety;
118 But he that tempered thee bade thee stand up,
119 Gave thee no instance why thou shouldst do treason,
120 Unless to dub thee with the name of traitor.
121 If that same demon that hath gulled thee thus
    Should with his lion gait walk the whole world,
123 He might return to vasty Tartar back
    And tell the legions, "I can never win
    A soul so easy as that Englishman's."
126 O, how hast thou with jealousy infected
127 The sweetness of affiance! Show men dutiful?
    Why, so didst thou. Seem they grave and learnèd?
    Why, so didst thou. Come they of noble family?
130 Why, so didst thou. Seem they religious?
    Why, so didst thou. Or are they spare in diet,
    Free from gross passion or of mirth or anger,
133 Constant in spirit, not swerving with the blood,
134 Garnished and decked in modest complement,
135 Not working with the eye without the ear,

107–8 *Working . . . them* i.e., cooperating with such obvious fitness as to provoke no cry of wonder   109 *proportion* fitness   110 *wait on* attend   112 *wrought upon* i.e., with a spell or infernal suggestion; *preposterously* abnormally   113 *voice* vote (?)   114 *suggest* tempt   115–17 *Do botch . . . piety* i.e., trick out sin with disguises of shining virtue   118 *tempered* molded; *stand up* rebel   119 *instance* excuse, example   120 *dub . . . name* acquire the title   121 *gulled* deceived   123 *Tartar* Tartarus (deepest Hades)   126 *jealousy* suspicion   127 *affiance* trust   133 *blood* passions   134 *decked . . . complement* i.e., wearing the look of modesty   135–36 *Not . . . neither* i.e., judiciously trusting neither eye nor ear alone

And but in purgèd judgment trusting neither?
Such and so finely bolted didst thou seem;   137
And thus thy fall hath left a kind of blot
To mark the full-fraught man and best indued   139
With some suspicion. I will weep for thee;   140
For this revolt of thine, methinks, is like
Another fall of man. Their faults are open.
Arrest them to the answer of the law;
And God acquit them of their practices!

EXETER   I arrest thee of high treason by the name of
Richard Earl of Cambridge.
 I arrest thee of high treason by the name of Henry
Lord Scroop of Masham.
 I arrest thee of high treason by the name of Thomas
Grey, knight, of Northumberland.   150

SCROOP
Our purposes God justly hath discovered,
And I repent my faults more than my death,
Which I beseech your highness to forgive,
Although my body pay the price of it.

CAMBRIDGE
For me, the gold of France did not seduce,
Although I did admit it as a motive   156
The sooner to effect what I intended.
But God be thankèd for prevention,
Which I in sufferance heartily will rejoice,   159
Beseeching God, and you, to pardon me.   160

GREY
Never did faithful subject more rejoice
At the discovery of most dangerous treason
Than I do at this hour joy o'er myself,
Prevented from a damnèd enterprise.
My fault, but not my body, pardon, sovereign.

---

137 *bolted* sifted (like flour)   139 *full-fraught . . . indued* most richly en-
dowed   156 *did admit* allowed to stand (Cambridge's historical "motive"
was to advance the dynastic claim of Edmund Mortimer, his father-in-law)
159 *sufferance* suffering

KING

166   God quit you in his mercy! Hear your sentence.
       You have conspired against our royal person,
       Joined with an enemy proclaimed, and from his coffers
169   Received the golden earnest of our death;
170   Wherein you would have sold your king to slaughter,
       His princes and his peers to servitude,
       His subjects to oppression and contempt,
       And his whole kingdom into desolation.
174   Touching our person, seek we no revenge,
175   But we our kingdom's safety must so tender,
       Whose ruin you have sought, that to her laws
       We do deliver you. Get you therefore hence,
       Poor miserable wretches, to your death;
       The taste whereof God of his mercy give
180   You patience to endure and true repentance
181   Of all your dear offenses! Bear them hence.
                    Exit [Guard, with Cambridge, Scroop, and Grey].
       Now, lords, for France; the enterprise whereof
183   Shall be to you as us, like glorious.
       We doubt not of a fair and lucky war,
       Since God so graciously hath brought to light
       This dangerous treason, lurking in our way
       To hinder our beginnings. We doubt not now
188   But every rub is smoothèd on our way.
       Then forth, dear countrymen. Let us deliver
190   Our puissance into the hand of God,
191   Putting it straight in expedition.
192   Cheerly to sea the signs of war advance.
       No king of England, if not King of France!
                                    Flourish. [Exeunt.]

                          *

---

166 *quit* acquit, forgive   **169** *earnest* advance payment   **174** *Touching* as re-
gards   **175** *tender* hold dear   **181** *dear* grievous (see ll. 58–60)   **183** *like*
alike   **188** *But* but that; *rub* obstacle   **191** *straight in expedition* immedi-
ately in motion   **192** *signs* ensigns, or flags

∾ **II.3** *Enter Pistol, Nym, Bardolph, Boy, and Hostess.*

HOSTESS   Prithee, honey-sweet husband, let me bring
   thee to Staines.   2
PISTOL
   No; for my manly heart doth earn.   3
   Bardolph, be blithe; Nym, rouse thy vaunting veins;
   Boy, bristle thy courage up; for Falstaff he is dead,
   And we must earn therefore.   6
BARDOLPH   Would I were with him, wheresome'er he is,
   either in heaven or in hell!
HOSTESS   Nay sure, he's not in hell! He's in Arthur's   9
   bosom, if ever man went to Arthur's bosom. 'A made a   10
   finer end, and went away an it had been any christom   11
   child. 'A parted ev'n just between twelve and one, ev'n
   at the turning o' th' tide. For after I saw him fumble
   with the sheets, and play with flowers, and smile upon
   his finger's end, I knew there was but one way; for his
   nose was as sharp as a pen, and 'a babbled of green   16
   fields. "How now, Sir John?" quoth I. "What, man? be
   o' good cheer." So 'a cried out "God, God, God!" three
   or four times. Now I, to comfort him, bid him 'a
   should not think of God; I hoped there was no need to   20
   trouble himself with any such thoughts yet. So 'a bade
   me lay more clothes on his feet. I put my hand into the
   bed and felt them, and they were as cold as any stone.
   Then I felt to his knees, and so upward and upward,
   and all was as cold as any stone.   25
NYM   They say he cried out of sack.   26
HOSTESS   Ay, that 'a did.

II.3 A London street   2 *Staines* (place on the road to Southampton)   **3, 6**
earn grieve (with puns on "yearn" and "get money," respectively)   **9** *Arthur's*
(confused with Abraham)   **10** *'A* he   **11** *christom* newly baptized   **16–17**
'a . . . fields (the folio has "an Table" for "babbled"; Theobald's emendation
proposes the vision of Falstaff's recitation of Psalm 23, apparently unknown
to the Hostess)   **25** *stone* (with wordplay on "testicle")   **26** *cried . . . sack* de-
nounced sack (a Spanish wine of which Falstaff was fond)

BARDOLPH   And of women.

HOSTESS   Nay, that 'a did not.

30 BOY   Yes, that 'a did, and said they were devils incarnate.

31 HOSTESS   'A could never abide carnation; 'twas a color he
never liked.

BOY   'A said once the devil would have him about
women.

35 HOSTESS   'A did in some sort, indeed, handle women;
36 but then he was rheumatic, and talked of the Whore of
Babylon.

BOY   Do you not remember 'a saw a flea stick upon Bardolph's nose, and 'a said it was a black soul burning in
40 hell?

41 BARDOLPH   Well, the fuel is gone that maintained that
fire. That's all the riches I got in his service.

43 NYM   Shall we shog? The king will be gone from
Southampton.

PISTOL
Come, let's away. My love, give me thy lips.
Look to my chattels and my movables.
47 Let senses rule. The word is "Pitch and pay."
Trust none;
49 For oaths are straws, men's faiths are wafer cakes,
50 And Hold-fast is the only dog, my duck.
51 Therefore Caveto be thy counselor.
52 Go, clear thy crystals. Yoke-fellows in arms,
Let us to France, like horse-leeches, my boys,
To suck, to suck, the very blood to suck!

BOY   And that's but unwholesome food, they say.

---

31 *carnation* (1) incarnation – see "incarnate," l.30, (2) whitish pink, the
color of some flesh   35 *handle* discuss (with pun on "manhandle" – i.e., as-
sault)   36 *rheumatic* i.e., feverish (perhaps with pronunciation "rom-atic,"
triggering the allusion to *Whore of Babylon* – i.e., the Roman Catholic
Church)   41 *fuel* i.e., liquor supplied by Falstaff   43 *shog* move along   47
Let . . . rule i.e., use your eyes and ears; *Pitch and pay* i.e., cash down   49
wafer cakes i.e., easily broken (proverbial)   50 *Hold-fast . . . dog* (from the
proverb "Brag is a good dog, but Hold-fast is a better")   51 *Caveto* beware
52 *clear thy crystals* wipe your eyes

PISTOL
    Touch her soft mouth, and march.
BARDOLPH   Farewell, hostess.
    [Kisses her.]
NYM   I cannot kiss, that is the humor of it; but adieu!
PISTOL
    Let housewifery appear. Keep close, I thee command.   59
HOSTESS   Farewell, adieu!   *Exeunt.* 60

*

∿ **II.4** *Flourish. Enter the French King, the Dauphin,*
the Dukes of Berri and Britaine[, the Constable, and
others].

KING
    Thus comes the English with full power upon us,
    And more than carefully it us concerns
    To answer royally in our defenses.
    Therefore the Dukes of Berri and Britaine,
    Of Brabant and of Orleans, shall make forth,
    And you, Prince Dauphin, with all swift dispatch,
    To line and new repair our towns of war   7
    With men of courage and with means defendant;
    For England his approaches makes as fierce
    As waters to the sucking of a gulf.   10
    It fits us then to be as provident
    As fear may teach us out of late examples   12
    Left by the fatal and neglected English   13
    Upon our fields.
DAUPHIN   My most redoubted father,
    It is most meet we arm us 'gainst the foe;   15
    For peace itself should not so dull a kingdom   16
    Though war nor no known quarrel were in question

---

59 *Let . . . appear* i.e., be a good housekeeper; *close* indoors
    II.4 Within the palace of the French king **7** *line* reinforce **10** *gulf*
whirlpool **12** *examples* i.e., of military defeats **13** *fatal and neglected* fatally
disregarded **15** *meet* fitting **16** *dull* blunt

But that defenses, musters, preparations
Should be maintained, assembled, and collected,
As were a war in expectation.
Therefore I say 'tis meet we all go forth
To view the sick and feeble parts of France;
And let us do it with no show of fear —
No, with no more than if we heard that England
Were busied with a Whitsun morris dance;
For, my good liege, she is so idly kinged,
Her scepter so fantastically borne,
By a vain, giddy, shallow, humorous youth,
That fear attends her not.

CONSTABLE   O peace, Prince Dauphin!
You are too much mistaken in this king.
Question your grace the late ambassadors,
With what great state he heard their embassy,
How well supplied with noble counselors,
How modest in exception, and withal
How terrible in constant resolution,
And you shall find his vanities forespent
Were but the outside of the Roman Brutus,
Covering discretion with a coat of folly;
As gardeners do with ordure hide those roots
That shall first spring and be most delicate.

DAUPHIN
Well, 'tis not so, my Lord High Constable.
But though we think it so, it is no matter.
In cases of defense 'tis best to weigh
The enemy more mighty than he seems.
So the proportions of defense are filled;
Which of a weak and niggardly projection

20
25
26
29
30
34
36
37
39
40
45
46

---

25 *Whitsun* Pentecost (Christian festival beginning fifty days after Easter
Sunday); *morris dance* folk dance including hobby horse   26 *idly* worthlessly
29 *attends* accompanies   34 *exception* taking issue   36 *forespent* now done
with   37 *Brutus* (Lucius Junius Brutus, who disguised his acumen from the
tyrant Tarquin Superbus until ready to join in revolt)   39 *ordure* compost,
manure   45 *proportions* adequate forces   46 *Which . . . projection* which defense, if skimped on or underestimated

Doth, like a miser, spoil his coat with scanting
A little cloth.
KING   Think we King Harry strong;
And, princes, look you strongly arm to meet him.
The kindred of him hath been fleshed upon us;   50
And he is bred out of that bloody strain
That haunted us in our familiar paths.
Witness our too much memorable shame
When Crécy battle fatally was struck,   54
And all our princes captived, by the hand
Of that black name, Edward, Black Prince of Wales;
Whiles that his mountain sire – on mountain standing,   57
Up in the air, crowned with the golden sun –
Saw his heroical seed, and smiled to see him   59
Mangle the work of nature, and deface   60
The patterns that by God and by French fathers   61
Had twenty years been made. This is a stem
Of that victorious stock; and let us fear
The native mightiness and fate of him.   64
    Enter a Messenger.
MESSENGER
Ambassadors from Harry King of England
Do crave admittance to your majesty.
KING
We'll give them present audience. Go, and bring them.
        [Exeunt Messenger and certain Lords.]
You see this chase is hotly followed, friends.
DAUPHIN
Turn head, and stop pursuit; for coward dogs   69
Most spend their mouths when what they seem to   70
    threaten
Runs far before them. Good my sovereign,
Take up the English short and let them know

---

50 *kindred* ancestors; *fleshed* initiated in blood shedding   **54** *Crécy* (French
defeat in 1346); *struck* waged   **57** *mountain* (1) huge, (2) born in mountainous Wales   **59** *seed* offspring   **61** *patterns* i.e., soldiers   **64** *fate* fortune,
luck   **69** *Turn head* stand at bay; *stop* i.e., put an end to   **70** *spend* . . .
mouths bark

Of what a monarchy you are the head.
Self-love, my liege, is not so vile a sin
As self-neglecting.
    Enter [Lords, with] Exeter [and train].

KING   From our brother of England?

EXETER

From him, and thus he greets your majesty:
He wills you, in the name of God Almighty,
That you divest yourself, and lay apart
The borrowed glories that by gift of heaven,
80   By law of nature and of nations, 'longs
To him and to his heirs – namely, the crown
82   And all wide-stretchèd honors that pertain
83   By custom, and the ordinance of times,
Unto the crown of France. That you may know
85   'Tis no sinister nor no awkward claim,
Picked from the wormholes of long-vanished days,
Nor from the dust of old oblivion raked,
88   He sends you this most memorable line,
    [Gives a paper.]
In every branch truly demonstrative;
90   Willing you overlook this pedigree;
91   And when you find him evenly derived
From his most famed of famous ancestors,
Edward the Third, he bids you then resign
94   Your crown and kingdom, indirectly held
95   From him, the native and true challenger.

KING

Or else what follows?

EXETER

97   Bloody constraint; for if you hide the crown
Even in your hearts, there will he rake for it.
Therefore in fierce tempest is he coming,

---

80 *By law . . . nations* i.e., morally and legally; *'longs* belongs 82 *all wide-stretchèd* i.e., the whole range of 83 *ordinance of times* tradition 85 *sinister* illegitimate; *awkward* shambling 88 *line* line of descent 91 *evenly* directly 94 *indirectly* wrongfully 95 *challenger* claimant 97 *constraint* force

In thunder and in earthquake, like a Jove;   100
That if requiring fail, he will compel;   101
And bids you, in the bowels of the Lord,   102
Deliver up the crown, and to take mercy
On the poor souls for whom this hungry war
Opens his vasty jaws; and on your head
Turning the widows' tears, the orphans' cries,   106
The dead men's blood, the privèd maidens' groans,   107
For husbands, fathers, and betrothèd lovers
That shall be swallowed in this controversy.
This is his claim, his threat'ning, and my message;   *110*
Unless the Dauphin be in presence here,
To whom expressly I bring greeting too.

KING
For us, we will consider of this further.
Tomorrow shall you bear our full intent
Back to our brother of England.

DAUPHIN   For the Dauphin,
I stand here for him. What to him from England?

EXETER
Scorn and defiance, slight regard, contempt,
And anything that may not misbecome
The mighty sender, doth he prize you at.   119
Thus says my king: and if your father's highness   *120*
Do not, in grant of all demands at large,
Sweeten the bitter mock you sent his majesty,
He'll call you to so hot an answer of it
That caves and womby vaultages of France   124
Shall chide your trespass, and return your mock
In second accent of his ordinance.   126

DAUPHIN
Say, if my father render fair return,
It is against my will; for I desire

---

100 *Jove* king of the gods   **101** *requiring* demanding   **102** *bowels* innermost being (see Phillipians 1 : 8) – hence, compassion   **106** *Turning* retorting, flinging back   **107** *privèd* deprived (i.e., of their "betrothèd lovers," l. 108) **119** *prize* esteem, value   **124** *womby vaultages* hollow caverns   **126** *second accent* i.e., echo; *ordinance* cannon

Nothing but odds with England. To that end,
130 As matching to his youth and vanity,
131 I did present him with the Paris balls.
EXETER
132 He'll make your Paris Louvre shake for it,
Were it the mistress court of mighty Europe;
And be assured you'll find a difference,
As we his subjects have in wonder found,
136 Between the promise of his greener days
137 And these he masters now. Now he weighs time
Even to the utmost grain. That you shall read
In your own losses, if he stay in France.
KING
140 Tomorrow shall you know our mind at full.
     Flourish.
EXETER
Dispatch us with all speed, lest that our king
Come here himself to question our delay;
143 For he is footed in this land already.
KING
You shall be soon dispatched with fair conditions.
A night is but small breath and little pause
To answer matters of this consequence.   *Exeunt.*
                    *

∾ **III.Cho.** *Enter Chorus.*

1 Thus with imagined wing our swift scene flies,
2 In motion of no less celerity
Than that of thought. Suppose that you have seen
4 The well-appointed king at Hampton pier
Embark his royalty; and his brave fleet
6 With silken streamers the young Phoebus fanning.

---

131 *Paris balls* tennis balls   132 *Louvre* royal palace   136 *greener* younger
137 *masters* governs   143 *footed* afoot
   III.Cho.   1 *imagined wing* wing of imagination   2 *celerity* quickness   4
well-appointed well-equipped   6 *Phoebus* the sun

Play with your fancies, and in them behold   7
Upon the hempen tackle shipboys climbing;
Hear the shrill whistle which doth order give
To sounds confused; behold the threaden sails,   10
Borne with th' invisible and creeping wind,
Draw the huge bottoms through the furrowed sea,   12
Breasting the lofty surge. O, do but think   13
You stand upon the rivage and behold   14
A city on th' inconstant billows dancing;
For so appears this fleet majestical,
Holding due course to Harfleur. Follow, follow!
Grapple your minds to sternage of this navy,   18
And leave your England as dead midnight still,
Guarded with grandsires, babies, and old women,   20
Either past or not arrived to pith and puissance;   21
For who is he whose chin is but enriched
With one appearing hair that will not follow
These culled and choice-drawn cavaliers to France?
Work, work your thoughts, and therein see a siege:
Behold the ordinance on their carriages,
With fatal mouths gaping on girded Harfleur.   27
Suppose th' ambassador from the French comes back;
Tells Harry that the king doth offer him
Katherine his daughter, and with her to dowry   30
Some petty and unprofitable dukedoms.
The offer likes not; and the nimble gunner   32
With linstock now the devilish cannon touches,   33
        Alarum, and chambers go off.
And down goes all before them. Still be kind,
And eke out our performance with your mind.   *Exit.*
                            *

---

7 *fancies* imaginations   10 *threaden* woven of thread   12 *bottoms* hulls   13
surge wave   14 *rivage* shore   18 *Grapple* fasten; *sternage* the sterns, or rear
ends, of boats   21 *pith* muscle, strength; *puissance* power   27 *girded* surrounded, besieged   32 *likes* pleases   33 *linstock* lighting stick **s.d.** *chambers*
small cannon (here firing blanks for a sound effect)

✺ **III.1** *Enter the King, Exeter, Bedford, and Gloucester.*
Alarum: [with Soldiers carrying] scaling ladders at
Harfleur.

KING

1   Once more unto the breach, dear friends, once more,
     Or close the wall up with our English dead!
     In peace there's nothing so becomes a man
     As modest stillness and humility,
     But when the blast of war blows in our ears,
     Then imitate the action of the tiger:
     Stiffen the sinews, summon up the blood,
     Disguise fair nature with hard-favored rage;
9   Then lend the eye a terrible aspect:
10   Let it pry through the portage of the head
     Like the brass cannon; let the brow o'erwhelm it
12   As fearfully as doth a gallèd rock
13   O'erhang and jutty his confounded base,
14   Swilled with the wild and wasteful ocean.
     Now set the teeth and stretch the nostril wide,
     Hold hard the breath and bend up every spirit
     To his full height! On, on, you noble English,
18   Whose blood is fet from fathers of war-proof,
19   Fathers that like so many Alexanders
20   Have in these parts from morn till even fought
21   And sheathed their swords for lack of argument.
22   Dishonor not your mothers; now attest
     That those whom you called fathers did beget you!
24   Be copy now to men of grosser blood
25   And teach them how to war! And you, good yeomen,

III.1 Before the walls of Harfleur 1 *breach* gap 9 *aspect* look 10 *portage*
portholes 12 *gallèd* eroded (at base) 13 *jutty his confounded* project over its
ruined 14 *Swilled* washed 18 *fet* fetched, derived; *war-proof* proven in war
19 *Alexanders* (Alexander III of Macedon [356–232 B.C.] was a great military
commander) 20 *even* evening 21 *argument* opposition 22 *attest* prove
24 *copy* examples; *grosser* less noble 25 *yeoman* (a rank below gentleman
knight)

Whose limbs were made in England, show us here
The mettle of your pasture. Let us swear   27
That you are worth your breeding; which I doubt not,
For there is none of you so mean and base   29
That hath not noble luster in your eyes.   30
I see you stand like greyhounds in the slips,   31
Straining upon the start. The game 's afoot!
Follow your spirit; and upon this charge
Cry "God for Harry, England and Saint George!"   34
              [Exeunt.] Alarum, and chambers go off.
                          *

∾ **III.2** *Enter Nym, Bardolph, Pistol, and Boy.*

BARDOLPH   On, on, on, on, on! to the breach, to the
  breach!
NYM   Pray thee, corporal, stay. The knocks are too hot;   3
  and, for mine own part, I have not a case of lives. The   4
  humor of it is too hot; that is the very plainsong of it.   5
PISTOL
  The plainsong is most just; for humors do abound.
  Knocks go and come; God's vassals drop and die;
              And sword and shield   8
              In bloody field
              Doth win immortal fame.   10
BOY   Would I were in an alehouse in London! I would
  give all my fame for a pot of ale and safety.
PISTOL   And I:
              If wishes would prevail with me,   14
              My purpose should not fail with me,
              But thither would I hie.

---

27 *mettle . . . pasture* quality of your rearing   29 *mean and base* lowly born
31 *slips* leashes   34 *Saint George* (England's patron saint)
    III.2. 3 *corporal* (at II.1.2 Bardolph was a lieutenant); *stay* wait   4 *case* set
5 *plainsong* unelaborated melody (i.e., unadorned truth)   8–10, 14–18
these may be lyric fragments and hence sung

BOY   As duly, but not as truly,
                       As bird doth sing on bough.
     Enter Fluellen.

19 FLUELLEN   Up to the preach, you dogs! Avaunt, you cul-
20   lions!
        [Drives them in.]
     PISTOL

21   Be merciful, great duke, to men of mold!
      Abate thy rage, abate thy manly rage,
      Abate thy rage, great duke!

24   Good bawcock, bate thy rage! Use lenity, sweet chuck!

25 NYM   These be good humors. Your honor wins bad
      humors.   *Exit [with all but Boy].*

     BOY   As young as I am, I have observed these three
28   swashers. I am boy to them all three; but all they three,
      though they would serve me, could not be man to me;
30   for indeed three such antics do not amount to a man.
31   For Bardolph, he is white-livered and red-faced; by the
32   means whereof 'a faces it out, but fights not. For Pistol,
      he hath a killing tongue and a quiet sword; by the
34   means whereof 'a breaks words and keeps whole
      weapons. For Nym, he hath heard that men of few
      words are the best men, and therefore he scorns to say
      his prayers, lest 'a should be thought a coward; but his
      few bad words are matched with as few good deeds, for
      'a never broke any man's head but his own, and that
40   was against a post when he was drunk. They will steal
41   anything, and call it purchase. Bardolph stole a lute-
      case, bore it twelve leagues, and sold it for three half-
      pence. Nym and Bardolph are sworn brothers in

---

19 *preach* (throughout, Fluellen substitutes "p" for "b" and "f" for "v," a
habit – and typography – meant to convey his Welsh pronunciation of English); *Avaunt* begone; *cullions* low types (originally, testicles) 21 *men of
mold* mere mortals 24 *bawcock* fine fellow 25 *These* i.e., lenity, abated
rage; *Your honor* i.e., Fluellen (who is angry – i.e., bad-humored) 28 *swashers* swashbucklers 30 *antics* fantastics, zanies 31 *white-livered* cowardly
32 *faces it out* puts on a brave front 34 *breaks words* (1) lies, (2) mangles language, (3) talks excessively 41 *purchase* (slang for stolen goods)

filching, and in Calais they stole a fire-shovel. I knew
by that piece of service the men would carry coals.   45
They would have me as familiar with men's pockets as
their gloves or their handkerchers; which makes much   47
against my manhood, if I should take from another's
pocket to put into mine; for it is plain pocketing up of
wrongs. I must leave them and seek some better service.   50
Their villainy goes against my weak stomach, and
therefore I must cast it up.   *Exit.*   52
    Enter Gower [and Fluellen].

GOWER Captain Fluellen, you must come presently to
the mines. The Duke of Gloucester would speak with   54
you.

FLUELLEN To the mines? Tell you the duke, it is not so
good to come to the mines; for look you, the mines is
not according to the disciplines of the war. The concav-   58
ities of it is not sufficient; for look you, th' athversary,
you may discuss unto the duke, look you, is digt him-   60
self four yard under the countermines. By Cheshu, I   61
think 'a will plow up all, if there is not petter direc-   62
tions.

GOWER The Duke of Gloucester, to whom the order of
the siege is given, is altogether directed by an Irishman,
a very valiant gentleman, i' faith.

FLUELLEN It is Captain Macmorris, is it not?

GOWER I think it be.

FLUELLEN By Cheshu, he is an ass as in the orld! I will
verify as much in his peard. He has no more directions   70
in the true disciplines of the wars, look you, of the
Roman disciplines, than is a puppy-dog.
    Enter Macmorris and Captain Jamy.

GOWER Here 'a comes, and the Scots captain, Captain
Jamy, with him.

---

45 *carry coals* i.e., put up with abuse   47 *makes* i.e., offends   52 *cast* vomit
54 *mines* tunneling operations   58 *disciplines* i.e., correct procedure; *concav-
ities* i.e., slope, downward pitch   61 *Cheshu* Jesu   62 *plow* blow   70 *in his
peard* in his beard, i.e., to his face; *directions* instructions

FLUELLEN   Captain Jamy is a marvelous falorous gentle-
76 man, that is certain, and of great expedition and
77 knowledge in th' aunchient wars, upon my particular
knowledge of his directions. By Cheshu, he will maintain his argument as well as any military man in the
80 orld in the disciplines of the pristine wars of the Ro-
mans.

JAMY   I say gud day, Captain Fluellen.

FLUELLEN   God-den to your worship, good Captain
James.

GOWER   How now, Captain Macmorris? Have you quit
86 the mines? Have the pioneers given o'er?

MACMORRIS   By Chrish, law, tish ill done! The work ish
give over, the trompet sound the retreat. By my hand I
swear, and my father's soul, the work ish ill done! It ish
90 give over. I wuld have blowed up the town, so Chrish
save me, law, in an hour. O, tish ill done! tish ill done!
By my hand, tish ill done!

FLUELLEN   Captain Macmorris, I beseech you now, will
94 you voutsafe me, look you, a few disputations with
you, as partly touching or concerning the disciplines of
the war, the Roman wars? In the way of argument, look
97 you, and friendly communication; partly to satisfy my
opinion, and partly for the satisfaction, look you, of my
mind, as touching the direction of the military disci-
100 pline, that is the point.

JAMY   It sall be vary gud, gud feith, gud captens bath,
102 and I sall quit you with gud leve, as I may pick occasion. That sall I, mary.

MACMORRIS   It is no time to discourse, so Chrish save
me! The day is hot, and the weather, and the wars, and
the king, and the dukes. It is no time to discourse. The
107 town is beseeched, and the trompet call us to the

---

76 *expedition* readiness   77 *aunchient* ancient   80 *pristine* primitive, ancient
86 *pioneers* sappers, diggers   94 *voutsafe* vouchsafe: allow, permit   97 *communication* consultation   102 *quit* answer   107 *beseeched* (1) besieged, (2)
begged

breach, and we talk, and, be Chrish, do nothing. 'Tis
shame for us all. So God sa' me, 'tis shame to stand still,
it is shame, by my hand! and there is throats to be cut,   *110*
and works to be done, and there ish nothing done, so
Chrish sa' me, law!   *112*

JAMY   By the mess, ere theise eyes of mine take them-   *113*
selves to slomber, ay'll de gud service, or ay'll lig i' th'   *114*
grund for it! ay, or go to death! And ay'll pay't as valor-
ously as I may, that sall I suerly do, that is the breff and
the long. Marry, I wad full fain heard some question   *117*
'tween you tway.

FLUELLEN   Captain Macmorris, I think, look you, under
your correction, there is not many of your nation –   *120*

MACMORRIS   Of my nation? What ish my nation? Ish a   *121*
villain and a bastard, and a knave, and a rascal! What
ish my nation? Who talks of my nation?

FLUELLEN   Look you, if you take the matter otherwise
than is meant, Captain Macmorris, peradventure I
shall think you do not use me with that affability as in
discretion you ought to use me, look you, being as
good a man as yourself, poth in the disciplines of war,
and in the derivation of my pirth, and in other particu-
larities.   *130*

MACMORRIS   I do not know you so good a man as myself. So Chrish save me, I will cut off your head!

GOWER   Gentlemen both, you will mistake each other.   *133*

JAMY   A', that's a foul fault!   *134*

   A parley [sounded].

GOWER   The town sounds a parley.

FLUELLEN   Captain Macmorris, when there is more petter opportunity to be required, look you, I will be so
pold as to tell you I know the disciplines of war; and
there is an end.   *Exit [with others].*

---

112 *law* la (an intensifying interjection)   113 *mess* i.e., Mass   114 *ay'll de*
I'll do; *lig* lie   117 *Marry* indeed; *fain* rather; *question* discussion   121
What ish what about; *Ish* he (whoever speaks disparagingly of Ireland)   133
will mistake persist in misjudging   134 *A'* (equivalent to "Ach")

*

✺ **III.3** *Enter the King [Henry] and all his train before the gates.*

KING
    How yet resolves the governor of the town?
2   This is the latest parle we will admit:
    Therefore to our best mercy give yourselves,
4   Or like to men proud of destruction
    Defy us to our worst; for as I am a soldier,
    A name that in my thoughts becomes me best,
7   If I begin the battery once again,
    I will not leave the half-achievèd Harfleur
    Till in her ashes she lie burièd.
10   The gates of mercy shall be all shut up,
11   And the fleshed soldier, rough and hard of heart,
12   In liberty of bloody hand shall range
13   With conscience wide as hell, mowing like grass
    Your fresh fair virgins and your flow'ring infants.
    What is it then to me if impious war,
    Arrayed in flames like to the prince of fiends,
17   Do with his smirched complexion all fell feats
    Enlinked to waste and desolation?
    What is't to me, when you yourselves are cause,
20   If your pure maidens fall into the hand
21   Of hot and forcing violation?
    What rein can hold licentious wickedness
23   When down the hill he holds his fierce career?
24   We may as bootless spend our vain command
    Upon th' enragèd soldiers in their spoil

III.3 Before the walls of Harfleur at the gates **2** *latest* final; *parle* parley, negotiation **4** *proud of* who glory in **7** *battery* artillery fire, bombardment **11** *fleshed* hardened with killing **12** *In* with **13** *wide* permissive **17** *smirched* sooty; *fell* savage **21** *violation* rape **23** *holds . . . career* maintains his fierce gallop **24** *bootless* uselessly

As send precepts to the leviathan   26
To come ashore. Therefore, you men of Harfleur,
Take pity of your town and of your people
Whiles yet my soldiers are in my command,
Whiles yet the cool and temperate wind of grace   30
O'erblows the filthy and contagious clouds   31
Of heady murder, spoil, and villainy.   32
If not – why, in a moment look to see
The blind and bloody soldier with foul hand
Defile the locks of your shrill-shrieking daughters;   35
Your fathers taken by the silver beards,
And their most reverend heads dashed to the walls;
Your naked infants spitted upon pikes,
Whiles the mad mothers with their howls confused
Do break the clouds, as did the wives of Jewry   40
At Herod's bloody-hunting slaughtermen.   41
What say you? Will you yield, and this avoid?
Or, guilty in defense, be thus destroyed?   43
      Enter Governor [on the wall].

GOVERNOR
Our expectation hath this day an end.
The Dauphin, whom of succors we entreated,   45
Returns us that his powers are not yet ready   46
To raise so great a siege. Therefore, great king,   47
We yield our town and lives to thy soft mercy.
Enter our gates, dispose of us and ours,
For we no longer are defensible.   50

KING
Open your gates. Come, uncle Exeter,
Go you and enter Harfleur; there remain
And fortify it strongly 'gainst the French.
Use mercy to them all. For us, dear uncle,

---

26 *precepts* written summons; *leviathan* whale **30** *grace* mercy **31**
O'erblows outblows **32** *heady* headstrong **35** *locks* (1) hair, (2) chastity
40 *Jewry* Judea **41** (See Matthew 2 : 16–18 for an account of Herod's
slaughter of the innocents) **43** *in defense* i.e., of reckless defense **45** *of succors* for aid, reinforcements **46** *Returns us* replies **47** *raise* defeat, break

The winter coming on, and sickness growing
Upon our soldiers, we will retire to Calais.
Tonight in Harfleur will we be your guest;
58 Tomorrow for the march are we addressed.
> *Flourish, and enter the town.*

*

∾ **III.4** *Enter Katherine and [Alice,] an old
Gentlewoman.*

KATHERINE Alice, tu as esté en Angleterre, et tu bien
parles le langage.

ALICE Un peu, madame.

KATHERINE Je te prie m'enseigner; il faut que j'apprends
à parler. Comment appelez-vous le main en Anglois?

ALICE Le main? Il est appelé de hand.

KATHERINE De hand. Et les doigts?

ALICE Les doigts? Ma foi, j'oublie les doigts; mais je me
souviendrai. Les doigts? Je pense qu'ils ont appelé de
10 fingres; oui, de fingres.

KATHERINE Le main, de hand; les doigts, de fingres. Je
pense que je suis le bon escolier; j'ai gagné deux mots
d'Anglois vistement. Comment appelez-vous les ongles?

ALICE Les ongles, les appelons de nailès.

KATHERINE De nailès. Escoute; dites-moi si je parle
bien: de hand, de fingres, et de nailès.

ALICE C'est bien dict, madame; il est fort bon Anglois.

KATHERINE Dites-moi l'Anglois pour le bras.

---

58 *addressed* prepared

III.4 Within the palace of the French king KATH. Alice, you have been in
England, and you speak the language well. AL. A little, my lady. KATH. I beg
you teach me; I must learn to speak it. What do you call *le main* in English?
AL. *Le main?* It is called *de hand.* KATH. *De hand.* And *les doigts?* AL. *Les doigts?*
My faith, I forget *les doigts;* but I will remember. *Les doigts?* I think they are
called *de fingres;* yes, *de fingres.* KATH. *Le main, de hand; les doigts, de fingres.* I
think I am a good scholar; I have learned two words of English quickly.
What do you call *les ongles?* AL. *Les ongles* we call *de nailès.* KATH. *De nailès.*
Listen; tell me if I speak well: *de hand, de fingres,* and *de nailès.* AL. Well spoken, my lady; it is very good English. KATH. Tell me the English for *le bras.*

ALICE   De arm, madame.

KATHERINE   Et le coude.   20

ALICE   D' elbow.

KATHERINE   D' elbow. Je me'en fais le répétition de tous les mots que vous m'avez apprins dès à présent.

ALICE   Il est trop difficile, madame, comme je pense.

KATHERINE   Excuse moi, Alice; escoute: d' hand, de fingre, de nailès, d' arma, de bilbow.

ALICE   D' elbow, madame.

KATHERINE   O Seigneur Dieu, je m'en oublie d' elbow! Comment appelez-vous le col?

ALICE   De nick, madame.   30

KATHERINE   De nick. Et le menton?

ALICE   De chin.

KATHERINE   De sin. Le col, de nick; le menton, de sin.

ALICE   Oui. Sauf vostre honneur, en vérité, vous prononcez les mots aussi droict que les natifs d'Angleterre.

KATHERINE   Je ne doute point d'apprendre, par la grace de Dieu, et en peu de temps.

ALICE   N'avez-vous pas déjà oublié ce que je vous ai enseigné?

KATHERINE   Non, je réciterai à vous promptement: 40
d' hand, de fingre, de mailès –

ALICE   De nailès, madame.

KATHERINE   De nailès, de arm, de ilbow –

ALICE   Sauf vostre honneur, d' elbow.

KATHERINE   Ainsi dis-je; d' elbow, de nick, et de sin. Comment appelez-vous le pied et la robe?

AL. *De arm,* my lady. KATH. And *le coude.* AL. *D' elbow.* KATH. *D' elbow.* I am going to repeat all the words you have taught me so far. AL. It is too hard, my lady, so I think. KATH. Excuse me, Alice; listen: *d' hand, de fingre, de nailès, d' arma, de bilbow.* AL. *D' elbow,* my lady. KATH. O Lord God, I can't remember *d' elbow.* What do you call *le col?* AL. *De nick,* my lady. KATH. *De nick.* And *le menton?* AL. *De chin.* KATH. *De sin. Le col, de nick; le menton, de sin.* AL. Yes. Save your honor, indeed you pronounce the words as well as the native English. KATH. I trust to learn, by the grace of God, and in short time. AL. You have not already forgotten what I have taught you? KATH. No. I shall recite for you promptly: *d' hand, de fingre, de mailès –* AL. *De nailès,* my lady. KATH. *De nailès, de arm, de ilbow –* AL. Save your honor, *d' elbow.* KATH. So I said – *d' elbow, de nick,* and *de sin.* What do you call *le pied* and *la robe?*

ALICE   De foot, madame; et de count.

KATHERINE   De foot et de count! O Seigneur Dieu! il-
s'ont les mots de son mauvais, corruptible, gros, et im-
50   pudique, et non pour les dames d'honneur d'user: je ne
voudrais prononcer ces mots devant les seigneurs de
France pour tout le monde. Foh! de foot et de count!
Néantmoins, je réciterai une autre fois ma leçon en-
semble: d' hand, de fingre, de nailès, d' arm, d' elbow,
de nick, de sin, de foot, de count.

ALICE   Excellent, madame!

KATHERINE   C'est assez pour une fois: allons-nous à
diner.   *Exit [with Alice].*

*

☙ III.5 *Enter the King of France, the Dauphin*
[, Britaine], the Constable of France, and others.

KING

1   'Tis certain he hath passed the river Somme.

CONSTABLE

And if he be not fought withal, my lord,
Let us not live in France; let us quit all
And give our vineyards to a barbarous people.

DAUPHIN

5   O Dieu vivant! Shall a few sprays of us,
6   The emptying of our fathers' luxury,

AL. *De foot,* my lady; and *de count* [i.e., gown]. KATH. *De foot* [which she mis-
takes for *"foutre"* – i.e., to fuck; and *"count"* or *"con,"* i.e., cunt, in English]. O
Lord God! they are bad words, wicked, coarse, and immodest, and not for
ladies of honor to use: I would not speak those words before the gentlemen
of France for all the world. Foh! *de foot* and *de count!* Nevertheless, I will recite once more my entire lesson: *d' hand, de fingre, de nailès, d' arm, d' elbow,
de nick, de sin, de foot, de count.* AL. Excellent, my lady! KATH. That's enough
for one time; let's go to dinner.
  III.5 The French king's quarters at Rouen   1 *passed . . . Somme* (in the
withdrawal to Calais)   5 *Dieu vivant* living God; *sprays* offshoots (i.e., the
English)   6 *fathers' luxury* i.e., forefathers' lust

Our scions, put in wild and savage stock,   7
Spurt up so suddenly into the clouds
And overlook their grafters?   9

BRITAINE

Normans, but bastard Normans, Norman bastards!   10
Mort de ma vie! if they march along   11
Unfought withal, but I will sell my dukedom
To buy a slobb'ry and a dirty farm   13
In that nook-shotten isle of Albion.   14

CONSTABLE

Dieu de batailles! where have they this mettle?   15
Is not their climate foggy, raw, and dull,
On whom, as in despite, the sun looks pale,   17
Killing their fruit with frowns? Can sodden water,   18
A drench for surreined jades, their barley broth,   19
Decoct their cold blood to such valiant heat?   20
And shall our quick blood, spirited with wine,   21
Seem frosty? O, for honor of our land,
Let us not hang like roping icicles   23
Upon our houses' thatch, whiles a more frosty people
Sweat drops of gallant youth in our rich fields –
"Poor" we call them in their native lords!   26

DAUPHIN

By faith and honor,
Our madams mock at us and plainly say   28
Our mettle is bred out, and they will give
Their bodies to the lust of English youth   *30*
To new-store France with bastard warriors.   31

---

7 *scions* grafts; *put in* grafted upon 9 *overlook* (1) stand taller than, (2) dominate 10 *Normans* (denizens of northwestern France and conquerors of England in 1066; hence Henry's people are "bastard" Normans) 11 *Mort . . . vie* death of my life 13 *slobb'ry* slovenly 14 *nook-shotten* full of nooks – i.e., with a ragged coastline 15 *batailles* battles 17 *despite* spite 18 *sodden* boiled 19 *drench . . . jades* draft for exhausted horses; *barley broth* ale (sometimes used as a drench) 20 *Decoct* infuse, warm 21 *quick* lively 23 *roping* spun out by dripping 26 *"Poor" . . . lords* i.e., but not rich in their possessors 28–29 *Our . . . out* our vigor has been diluted (presumably by inbreeding) 31 *new-store* resupply

BRITAINE
>   They bid us to the English dancing schools
33   And teach lavoltas high, and swift corantos,
34   Saying our grace is only in our heels
>   And that we are most lofty runaways.

KING
>   Where is Montjoy the herald? Speed him hence;
>   Let him greet England with our sharp defiance.
>   Up, princes! and with spirit of honor edged
>   More sharper than your swords, hie to the field.
40   Charles Delabreth, High Constable of France,
>   You Dukes of Orleans, Bourbon, and of Berri,
>   Alençon, Brabant, Bar, and Burgundy;
>   Jacques Chatillon, Rambures, Vaudemont,
>   Beaumont, Grandpré, Roussi, and Faulconbridge,
>   Foix, Lestrale, Bouciqualt, and Charolois,
>   High dukes, great princes, barons, lords, and knights,
47   For your great seats now quit you of great shames.
>   Bar Harry England, that sweeps through our land
49   With pennons painted in the blood of Harfleur.
50   Rush on his host as doth the melted snow
51   Upon the valleys whose low vassal seat
52   The Alps doth spit and void his rheum upon.
>   Go down upon him – you have power enough –
54   And in a captive chariot into Rouen
>   Bring him our prisoner.

CONSTABLE   This becomes the great.
>   Sorry am I his numbers are so few,
>   His soldiers sick and famished in their march;
>   For I am sure, when he shall see our army,
59   He'll drop his heart into the sink of fear
60   And, for achievement, offer us his ransom.

---

33 *And* i.e., to; *lavoltas* dances characterized by leaps; *corantos* i.e., dances characterized by running steps 34 *in our heels* (1) as dancers, (2) as those who "take to their heels" 47 *quit* acquit 49 *pennons* flags 51 *vassal* slavish 52 *rheum* phlegm – i.e., waters 54 *captive chariot* i.e., vehicle to carry the captured Henry 59 *sink* pit 60 *for achievement* i.e., instead of conquering

KING
>Therefore, Lord Constable, haste on Montjoy,
>And let him say to England that we send
>To know what willing ransom he will give.
>Prince Dauphin, you shall stay with us in Rouen.

DAUPHIN
>Not so, I do beseech your majesty.

KING
>Be patient, for you shall remain with us.
>Now forth, Lord Constable and princes all,
>And quickly bring us word of England's fall.   *Exeunt.*

*

∾ **III.6** *Enter Captains, English and Welsh – Gower and*
Fluellen.

GOWER   How now, Captain Fluellen? Come you from
the bridge?

FLUELLEN   I assure you there is very excellent services
committed at the pridge.

GOWER   Is the Duke of Exeter safe?

FLUELLEN   The Duke of Exeter is as magnanimous as
Agamemnon, and a man that I love and honor with my   7
soul, and my heart, and my duty, and my live, and my   8
living, and my uttermost power. He is not – God be
praised and plessed! – any hurt in the orld, but keeps   10
the pridge most valiantly, with excellent discipline.
There is an aunchient lieutenant there at the pridge, I   12
think in my very conscience he is as valiant a man as
Mark Antony, and he is a man of no estimation in the   14
orld, but I did see him do as gallant service.

GOWER   What do you call him?

III.6 The English camp in Picardy   7 *Agamemnon* Greek leader in the Trojan War (a typically grandiose comparison)   8 *live* i.e., life   12 *aunchient
lieutenant* (Pistol is elsewhere ranked simply as "ancient," i.e., ensign)   14
Mark Antony Roman general; *estimation* fame

FLUELLEN   He is called Aunchient Pistol.

GOWER   I know him not.

> *Enter Pistol.*

FLUELLEN   Here is the man.

PISTOL

20   Captain, I thee beseech to do me favors.
The Duke of Exeter doth love thee well.

FLUELLEN   Ay, I praise God; and I have merited some
love at his hands.

PISTOL

Bardolph, a soldier firm and sound of heart,
25   And of buxom valor, hath by cruel fate,
And giddy Fortune's furious fickle wheel –
That goddess blind,
That stands upon the rolling restless stone –

FLUELLEN   By your patience, Aunchient Pistol. Fortune
30   is painted plind, with a muffler afore her eyes, to signify
to you that Fortune is plind; and she is painted also
with a wheel, to signify to you, which is the moral of it,
that she is turning and inconstant, and mutability, and
variation; and her foot, look you, is fixed upon a spher-
ical stone, which rolls, and rolls, and rolls. In good
truth, the poet makes a most excellent description of it.
37   Fortune is an excellent moral.

PISTOL

38   Fortune is Bardolph's foe, and frowns on him;
39   For he hath stolen a pax, and hangèd must 'a be –
40   A damnèd death!
Let gallows gape for dog; let man go free,
And let not hemp his windpipe suffocate.
43   But Exeter hath given the doom of death
For pax of little price.

---

25 *buxom* blithe, jolly   30 *muffler* blindfold   37 *moral* i.e., emblem of in-
struction (the goddess Fortune figured prominently in literary and pictorial
admonitions about the mutability of life)   38 *foe . . . frowns* (reminiscent of
popular ballad "Fortune, my foe, why dost thou frown on me?")   39 *pax*
(metal disk engraved with a crucifix, kissed during celebration of Mass)   43
doom sentence

Therefore, go speak – the duke will hear thy voice;
And let not Bardolph's vital thread be cut
With edge of penny cord and vile reproach.   47
Speak, captain, for his life, and I will thee requite.

FLUELLEN   Aunchient Pistol, I do partly understand your
meaning.   50

PISTOL
Why then, rejoice therefore!

FLUELLEN   Certainly, Aunchient, it is not a thing to rejoice at; for if, look you, he were my prother, I would
desire the duke to use his good pleasure and put him to
execution; for discipline ought to be used.

PISTOL
Die and be damned! and figo for thy friendship!   56

FLUELLEN   It is well.

PISTOL
The fig of Spain!   *Exit.*

FLUELLEN   Very good.

GOWER   Why, this is an arrant counterfeit rascal! I re-   60
member him now – a bawd, a cutpurse.

FLUELLEN   I'll assure you, 'a uttered as prave words at the
pridge as you shall see in a summer's day. But it is very
well. What he has spoke to me, that is well, I warrant
you, when time is serve.

GOWER   Why, 'tis a gull, a fool, a rogue, that now and   66
then goes to the wars to grace himself, at his return into
London, under the form of a soldier. And such fellows
are perfit in the great commanders' names, and they   69
will learn you by rote where services were done: at such   70
and such a sconce, at such a breach, at such a convoy;   71
who came off bravely, who was shot, who disgraced,
what terms the enemy stood on; and this they con per-   73
fitly in the phrase of war, which they trick up with new-

---

47 *penny cord* cheap rope   56 *figo* i.e., Spanish for fig (epithet and gesture of
contempt made by thrusting thumb between index and middle finger)   66
gull dupe, rascal   69 *perfit* word perfect   71 *sconce* earthwork, fortification;
convoy transport of troops   73 *con* learn

tuned oaths; and what a beard of the general's cut and a
76 horrid suit of the camp will do among foaming bottles
and ale-washed wits is wonderful to be thought on. But
78 you must learn to know such slanders of the age, or else
you may be marvelously mistook.

80 FLUELLEN   I tell you what, Captain Gower, I do perceive
he is not the man that he would gladly make show to
82 the orld he is. If I find a hole in his coat, I will tell him
my mind. *[Drum within.]* Hark you, the king is coming, and I must speak with him from the pridge.

Drum and Colors. Enter the King and his poor
Soldiers [and Gloucester].

God pless your majesty!

KING
How now, Fluellen? Cam'st thou from the bridge?

FLUELLEN   Ay, so please your majesty. The Duke of Exeter has very gallantly maintained the pridge; the
French is gone off, look you, and there is gallant and
90 most prave passages. Marry, th' athversary was have
possession of the pridge, but he is enforced to retire,
and the Duke of Exeter is master of the pridge. I can
tell your majesty, the duke is a prave man.

KING   What men have you lost, Fluellen?

95 FLUELLEN   The perdition of th' athversary hath been very
great, reasonable great. Marry, for my part, I think the
duke hath lost never a man but one that is like to be executed for robbing a church – one Pardolph, if your
99 majesty know the man. His face is all bubukles and
100 whelks, and knobs, and flames o' fire, and his lips plows
at his nose, and it is like a coal of fire, sometimes plue
and sometimes red; but his nose is executed, and his
fire's out.

KING   We would have all such offenders so cut off. And
we give express charge that in our marches through the

---

76 *horrid suit* rough or coarse attire   78 *slanders* disgraces   82 *a hole . . .*
coat i.e., a means of exposing him   90 *passages* (of arms)   95 *perdition* loss,
casualties   99–100 *bubukles and whelks* carbuncles and pimples

country there be nothing compelled from the villages, nothing taken but paid for; none of the French upbraided or abused in disdainful language; for when lenity and cruelty play for a kingdom, the gentler gamester is the soonest winner.   109   110

Tucket. Enter Montjoy.

MONTJOY   You know me by my habit.   111

KING   Well then, I know thee. What shall I know of thee?

MONTJOY   My master's mind.

KING   Unfold it.

MONTJOY   Thus says my king: Say thou to Harry of England: Though we seemed dead, we did but sleep. Advantage is a better soldier than rashness. Tell him we could have rebuked him at Harfleur, but that we thought not good to bruise an injury till it were full ripe. Now we speak upon our cue, and our voice is imperial. England shall repent his folly, see his weakness, and admire our sufferance. Bid him therefore consider of his ransom, which must proportion the losses we have borne, the subjects we have lost, the disgrace we have digested; which in weight to re-answer, his pettiness would bow under. For our losses, his exchequer is too poor; for th' effusion of our blood, the muster of his kingdom too faint a number; and for our disgrace, his own person kneeling at our feet but a weak and worthless satisfaction. To this add defiance; and tell him for conclusion he hath betrayed his followers, whose condemnation is pronounced. So far my king and master; so much my office.   118   120   123   124   126   130

KING

What is thy name? I know thy quality.   135

MONTJOY   Montjoy.

---

109 *lenity* leniency; *gentler* (1) more kind, (2) more noble   **110 s.d.** *Tucket* trumpet call   **111** *habit* attire   **118** *Advantage* circumspection   **120** *bruise* squeeze (as in treating a boil)   **123** *sufferance* patience   **124** *proportion* be equal to   **126–27** *which . . . under* i.e., to compensate for which his means are too small   **135** *quality* rank

KING
　　Thou dost thy office fairly. Turn thee back,
　　And tell thy king I do not seek him now,
　　But could be willing to march on to Calais
140　Without impeachment: for, to say the sooth,
　　Though 'tis no wisdom to confess so much
142　Unto an enemy of craft and vantage,
　　My people are with sickness much enfeebled,
　　My numbers lessened, and those few I have
　　Almost no better than so many French,
　　Who when they were in health, I tell thee, herald,
　　I thought upon one pair of English legs
　　Did march three Frenchmen. Yet forgive me, God,
　　That I do brag thus! This your air of France
150　Hath blown that vice in me. I must repent.
　　Go therefore tell thy master here I am;
　　My ransom is this frail and worthless trunk;
　　My army but a weak and sickly guard;
　　Yet, God before, tell him we will come on,
　　Though France himself and such another neighbor
　　Stand in our way. There's for thy labor, Montjoy.
　　　　[Gives a purse.]
157　Go bid thy master well advise himself:
　　If we may pass, we will; if we be hind'red,
　　We shall your tawny ground with your red blood
160　Discolor; and so, Montjoy, fare you well.
　　The sum of all our answer is but this:
　　We would not seek a battle as we are,
　　Nor, as we are, we say we will not shun it.
　　So tell your master.
MONTJOY
　　I shall deliver so. Thanks to your highness.　　　[Exit.]
GLOUCESTER
　　I hope they will not come upon us now.

_____

140 *impeachment* impediment　142 *vantage* superiority in numbers　150
blown brought to bloom　157 *advise himself* consider

KING
    We are in God's hand, brother, not in theirs.
    March to the bridge. It now draws toward night.
    Beyond the river we'll encamp ourselves,
    And on tomorrow bid them march away.   *Exeunt.* *170*

                    ✳

∾ **III.7** *Enter the Constable of France, the Lord
    Rambures, Orleans, Dauphin, with others.*

CONSTABLE   Tut! I have the best armor of the world.
    Would it were day!
ORLEANS   You have an excellent armor; but let my horse
    have his due.
CONSTABLE   It is the best horse of Europe.
ORLEANS   Will it never be morning?
DAUPHIN   My Lord of Orleans, and my Lord High Con-
    stable, you talk of horse and armor?
ORLEANS   You are as well provided of both as any prince
    in the world.   *10*
DAUPHIN   What a long night is this! I will not change my
    horse with any that treads but on four pasterns. Ça, ha!
    he bounds from the earth, as if his entrails were hairs; *13*
    le cheval volant, the Pegasus, chez les narines de feu!   *14*
    When I bestride him, I soar, I am a hawk. He trots the
    air. The earth sings when he touches it. The basest horn *16*
    of his hoof is more musical than the pipe of Hermes.   *17*
ORLEANS   He's of the color of the nutmeg.
DAUPHIN   And of the heat of the ginger. It is a beast for   *19*
    Perseus: he is pure air and fire; and the dull elements of *20*
    earth and water never appear in him, but only in pa-

III.7 The French camp near Agincourt   **13** *entrails* innards, intestines; *hairs*
(like the stuffing of a tennis ball)   **14** *le cheval . . . feu* the flying horse, Pegasus, with nostrils of fire   **16** *basest horn* (1) least part of the hoof, (2) hoof-
beat   **17** *pipe* (the musical instrument with which Hermes – i.e., Mercury –
lulled to sleep the monster Argus)   **19** *ginger* spicy root   **20** *Perseus* (in
Ovid, the rider of Pegasus while rescuing Andromeda from a dragon)

tient stillness while his rider mounts him. He is indeed
23 a horse, and all other jades you may call beasts.
24 CONSTABLE   Indeed, my lord, it is a most absolute and
excellent horse.
26 DAUPHIN   It is the prince of palfreys. His neigh is like the
bidding of a monarch, and his countenance enforces
homage.
ORLEANS   No more, cousin.
30 DAUPHIN   Nay, the man hath no wit that cannot, from
31 the rising of the lark to the lodging of the lamb, vary
deserved praise on my palfrey. It is a theme as fluent as
the sea. Turn the sands into eloquent tongues, and my
34 horse is argument for them all. 'Tis a subject for a sov-
35 ereign to reason on, and for a sovereign's sovereign to
ride on; and for the world, familiar to us and unknown,
37 to lay apart their particular functions and wonder at
him. I once writ a sonnet in his praise and began thus,
"Wonder of nature!"
40 ORLEANS   I have heard a sonnet begin so to one's mistress.
DAUPHIN   Then did they imitate that which I composed
43 to my courser, for my horse is my mistress.
44 ORLEANS   Your mistress bears well.
45 DAUPHIN   Me well, which is the prescript praise and per-
fection of a good and particular mistress.
CONSTABLE   Nay, for methought yesterday your mistress
48 shrewdly shook your back.
DAUPHIN   So perhaps did yours.
50 CONSTABLE   Mine was not bridled.

---

23 *jades* nags (also slang for whore: see l. 58)   24 *absolute* perfect   26 *palfreys* saddle horses   31 *lodging* i.e., going to bed   34 *argument* subject   35
reason discourse   37 *to lay . . . functions* i.e., to combine   43 *courser* horse
44 *bears* i.e., bears your weight sexually (the innuendo continues throughout
the exchange)   45 *prescript* appropriate   48 *shrewdly* (1) severely, (2)
shrewishly

DAUPHIN   O, then belike she was old and gentle, and you
rode like a kern of Ireland, your French hose off, and in 52
your strait strossers. 53

CONSTABLE   You have good judgment in horsemanship.

DAUPHIN   Be warned by me then. They that ride so, and
ride not warily, fall into foul bogs. I had rather have my 56
horse to my mistress. 57

CONSTABLE   I had as lief have my mistress a jade. 58

DAUPHIN   I tell thee, Constable, my mistress wears his
own hair. 60

CONSTABLE   I could make as true a boast as that, if I had
a sow to my mistress.

DAUPHIN   "Le chien est retourné à son propre vomisse- 63
ment, et la truie lavée au bourbier." Thou mak'st use of
anything.

CONSTABLE   Yet do I not use my horse for my mistress,
or any such proverb so little kin to the purpose.

RAMBURES   My Lord Constable, the armor that I saw in
your tent tonight – are those stars or suns upon it?

CONSTABLE   Stars, my lord. 70

DAUPHIN   Some of them will fall tomorrow, I hope.

CONSTABLE   And yet my sky shall not want. 72

DAUPHIN   That may be, for you bear a many superflu- 73
ously, and 'twere more honor some were away. 74

CONSTABLE   Ev'n as your horse bears your praises, who
would trot as well, were some of your brags dis-
mounted.

DAUPHIN   Would I were able to load him with his desert! 78
Will it never be day? I will trot tomorrow a mile, and
my way shall be paved with English faces. 80

---

52 *kern* Irish bush fighter; *French hose* breeches 53 *strait strossers* tight
trousers – i.e., bare-legged 56 *foul bogs* (1) Irish swamps, (2) repellent female genitalia 57 *to* as 58 *lief* rather 63–64 *Le chien . . . bourbier* the dog
is returned to his own vomit and the washed sow to the mire (II Peter 2 : 22)
72 *want* be lacking (in stars – i.e., honors) 73 *a many* i.e., many 74
'twere . . . away it were more fitting if some of your stars were done away
with 78 *desert* deservings

81 CONSTABLE   I will not say so, for fear I should be faced out of my way: but I would it were morning, for I would fain be about the ears of the English.

84 RAMBURES   Who will go to hazard with me for twenty prisoners?

CONSTABLE   You must first go yourself to hazard ere you have them.

DAUPHIN   'Tis midnight; I'll go arm myself.   *Exit.*

ORLEANS   The Dauphin longs for morning.

90 RAMBURES   He longs to eat the English.

CONSTABLE   I think he will eat all he kills.

ORLEANS   By the white hand of my lady, he's a gallant prince.

94 CONSTABLE   Swear by her foot, that she may tread out the oath.

ORLEANS   He is simply the most active gentleman of France.

98 CONSTABLE   Doing is activity, and he will still be doing.

99 ORLEANS   He never did harm, that I heard of.

100 CONSTABLE   Nor will do none tomorrow. He will keep that good name still.

ORLEANS   I know him to be valiant.

CONSTABLE   I was told that by one that knows him better than you.

ORLEANS   What's he?

CONSTABLE   Marry, he told me so himself, and he said he cared not who knew it.

108 ORLEANS   He needs not; it is no hidden virtue in him.

---

80 *faced* (1) shamed (for boasting), (2) turned away   **84** *go to hazard* play at dice   **94** *that* i.e., so that; *tread out* (1) stamp out, (2) fulfill by dancing, or sexual intercourse   **98** *Doing* (1) acting, (2) sexual intercourse; *still* continually   **99** *did harm* offended (the Constable uses it to mean "harm an enemy")   **108** *it* valor

CONSTABLE By my faith, sir, but it is! Never anybody 109
saw it but his lackey. 'Tis a hooded valor; and when it 110
appears, it will bate. 111

ORLEANS Ill will never said well.

CONSTABLE I will cap that proverb with "There is flat- 113
tery in friendship."

ORLEANS And I will take up that with "Give the devil his
due."

CONSTABLE Well placed! There stands your friend for 117
the devil. Have at the very eye of that proverb with "A 118
pox of the devil!" 119

ORLEANS You are the better at proverbs, by how much "a 120
fool's bolt is soon shot." 121

CONSTABLE You have shot over. 122

ORLEANS 'Tis not the first time you were overshot. 123

Enter a Messenger.

MESSENGER My Lord High Constable, the English lie
within fifteen hundred paces of your tents.

CONSTABLE Who hath measured the ground?

MESSENGER The Lord Grandpré.

CONSTABLE A valiant and most expert gentleman.
Would it were day! Alas, poor Harry of England! He
longs not for the dawning, as we do. 130

ORLEANS What a wretched and peevish fellow is this
king of England, to mope with his fat-brained follow- 132
ers so far out of his knowledge!

CONSTABLE If the English had any apprehension, they 134
would run away.

109–10 *Never . . . lackey* he is valiant only in beating his servant **110**
hooded with head covered – i.e., like a quiescent hawk **111** *bate* flutter –
i.e., like a hawk when unhooded (with pun on "bate" in sense of "diminish")
113 *cap* top (capping quotations, proverbs, etc., was a common pastime)
117 *Well placed* well played – i.e., appropriate **117–18** *stands . . . devil*
takes the place of **118** *Have . . . eye* i.e., right on the mark **119** *of* on **121**
bolt short arrow **122** *shot over* i.e., over the mark **123** *overshot* i.e., defeated **132** *mope* (1) stumble about, (2) be melancholy **134** *apprehension*
understanding

ORLEANS   That they lack; for if their heads had any intellectual armor, they could never wear such heavy headpieces.

RAMBURES   That island of England breeds very valiant
140   creatures. Their mastiffs are of unmatchable courage.

141   ORLEANS   Foolish curs, that run winking into the mouth of a Russian bear and have their heads crushed like rotten apples! You may as well say that's a valiant flea that dare eat his breakfast on the lip of a lion.

145   CONSTABLE   Just, just! and the men do sympathize with the mastiffs in robustious and rough coming on, leaving their wits and their wives; and then give them great meals of beef and iron and steel; they will eat like wolves and fight like devils.

150   ORLEANS   Ay, but these English are shrewdly out of beef.

CONSTABLE   Then shall we find tomorrow they have
152   only stomachs to eat and none to fight. Now is it time to arm. Come, shall we about it?

ORLEANS
It is now two o'clock; but let me see – by ten
We shall have each a hundred Englishmen.   *Exeunt.*

*

❧ **IV.Cho.** *Chorus.*

1   Now entertain conjecture of a time
2   When creeping murmur and the poring dark
Fills the wide vessel of the universe.
From camp to camp, through the foul womb of night,
5   The hum of either army stilly sounds,
6   That the fixed sentinels almost receive
The secret whispers of each other's watch.
8   Fire answers fire, and through their paly flames

---

141 *winking* with eyes shut   145 *Just* exactly; *sympathize* i.e., have fellow-feeling   150 *shrewdly* extremely   152 *stomachs* appetites
    IV. Cho.   1 *entertain conjecture of* imagine   2 *poring* necessary to peer in   5 *stilly* quietly   6 *That* so that   8 *paly* pale

Each battle sees the other's umbered face.   9
Steed threatens steed, in high and boastful neighs   *10*
Piercing the night's dull ear; and from the tents
The armorers accomplishing the knights,   12
With busy hammers closing rivets up,
Give dreadful note of preparation.
The country cocks do crow, the clocks do toll
And the third hour of drowsy morning name.
Proud of their numbers and secure in soul,   17
The confident and overlusty French   18
Do the low-rated English play at dice;   19
And chide the cripple tardy-gaited night   *20*
Who like a foul and ugly witch doth limp
So tediously away. The poor condemnèd English
Like sacrifices, by their watchful fires
Sit patiently and inly ruminate   24
The morning's danger; and their gesture sad,   25
Investing lank-lean cheeks and war-worn coats,   26
Presenteth them unto the gazing moon
So many horrid ghosts. O, now, who will behold   28
The royal captain of this ruined band
Walking from watch to watch, from tent to tent,   *30*
Let him cry, "Praise and glory on his head!"
For forth he goes and visits all his host,   32
Bids them good morrow with a modest smile
And calls them brothers, friends, and countrymen.
Upon his royal face there is no note
How dread an army hath enrounded him;   36
Nor doth he dedicate one jot of color   37
Unto the weary and all-watchèd night,   38
But freshly looks, and overbears attaint   39

---

9 *battle* army; *umbered* shadowed **12** *accomplishing* equipping **17** *secure in soul* confident in spirit **18** *overlusty* overlively **19** *play* i.e., play for **24** *inly* inwardly **25** *gesture* bearing; *sad* solemn **26** *Investing* carrying **28** *So* as so; *horrid* fearsome **32** *host* army **36** *dread* dreadful; *enrounded* surrounded **37** *dedicate* yield up; *color* complexion **38** *all-watchèd* wakeful **39** *overbears attaint* masters fatigue; or overcomes questions about his own legitimate right to the throne

40 With cheerful semblance and sweet majesty;
    That every wretch, pining and pale before,
    Beholding him, plucks comfort from his looks.
    A largess universal, like the sun.
    His liberal eye doth give to every one,
45 Thawing cold fear, that mean and gentle all
46 Behold, as may unworthiness define,
    A little touch of Harry in the night.
    And so our scene must to the battle fly;
    Where (O for pity!) we shall much disgrace
50 With four or five most vile and ragged foils,
    Right ill-disposed in brawl ridiculous,
    The name of Agincourt. Yet sit and see,
53 Minding true things by what their mockeries be.   *Exit.*

                            *

∾ **IV.1** *Enter the King, Bedford, and Gloucester.*

KING
    Gloucester, 'tis true that we are in great danger;
    The greater therefore should our courage be.
    Good morrow, brother Bedford. God Almighty!
    There is some soul of goodness in things evil,
5   Would men observingly distill it out;
    For our bad neighbor makes us early stirrers,
7   Which is both healthful, and good husbandry.
    Besides, they are our outward consciences,
    And preachers to us all, admonishing
10 That we should dress us fairly for our end.
    Thus may we gather honey from the weed
    And make a moral of the devil himself.
        Enter Erpingham.

---

40 *semblance* appearance   45 *mean and gentle* lowborn and highborn   46 *as . . . define* as it may be roughly expressed   50 *foils* swords   53 *Minding* bearing in mind; *mockeries* absurd imitations
    IV.1 The English camp near Agincourt   5 *Would* would that; *distill* discern   7 *husbandry* management   10 *dress us* prepare ourselves

Good morrow, old Sir Thomas Erpingham.
A good soft pillow for that good white head
Were better than a churlish turf of France.   15

ERPINGHAM
Not so, my liege. This lodging likes me better,   16
Since I may say, "Now lie I like a king."   17

KING
'Tis good for men to love their present pains
Upon example; so the spirit is eased.   19
And when the mind is quickened, out of doubt   20
The organs, though defunct and dead before,
Break up their drowsy grave and newly move   22
With casted slough and fresh legerity.   23
Lend me thy cloak, Sir Thomas. Brothers both,   24
Commend me to the princes in our camp;
Do my good morrow to them, and anon
Desire them all to my pavilion.

GLOUCESTER
We shall, my liege.

ERPINGHAM
Shall I attend your grace?

KING   No, my good knight.
Go with my brothers to my lords of England.   30
I and my bosom must debate awhile,   31
And then I would no other company.

ERPINGHAM
The Lord in heaven bless thee, noble Harry!
                           Exeunt [all but the King].

KING
God-a-mercy, old heart! thou speak'st cheerfully.
    Enter Pistol.

PISTOL   Che vous la?   35

---

15 *churlish* rough, ungentle   16 *likes* appeals to   17 *lie* (with pun on tell a falsehood?)   19 *Upon example* in exemplary fashion   20 *quickened* enlivened; *out of doubt* undoubtedly   22 *Break ... grave* break out of their grave of lethargy   23 *casted slough* discarded old skin; *legerity* briskness   24 *Brothers both* i.e., Bedford and Gloucester   31 *bosom* i.e., inner self, soul   35 *Che vous la* (Pistol's version of *"Qui va là,"* i.e., who goes there)

KING   A friend.

PISTOL

37   Discuss unto me, art thou officer;
38   Or art thou base, common, and popular?

39 KING   I am a gentleman of a company.

PISTOL

40   Trail'st thou the puissant pike?

    KING   Even so. What are you?

PISTOL

    As good a gentleman as the emperor.

    KING   Then you are a better than the king.

PISTOL

44   The king 's a bawcock, and a heart of gold,
45   A lad of life, an imp of fame,
      Of parents good, of fist most valiant.
47   I kiss his dirty shoe, and from heartstring
48   I love the lovely bully. What is thy name?

49 KING   Harry le Roy.

PISTOL

50   Le Roy? A Cornish name. Art thou of Cornish crew?

51 KING   No, I am a Welshman.

PISTOL

    Know'st thou Fluellen?

    KING   Yes.

PISTOL

54   Tell him I'll knock his leek about his pate
55   Upon Saint Davy's day.

    KING   Do not you wear your dagger in your cap that day,
    lest he knock that about yours.

---

37 *Discuss* declare 38 *popular* of low birth 39 *a gentleman . . . company* person of "gentle" (not "common") status serving as a volunteer 40 *Trail'st . . . pike* i.e., are you an infantryman 44 *bawcock* fine fellow (cf. III.2.24) 45 *imp* child 47 *heartstring* i.e., the very cords of my heart 48 *bully* (affectionate term meaning fine fellow) 49 *le Roy* i.e., with a pun on the French for "the king" *(le roi)* 51 *a Welshman* Henry, once Prince of Wales, was born at Monmouth in Wales 54 *leek* (onion-family vegetable worn to commemorate a Welsh victory, under Saint David, over the Saxons) 55 *Saint Davy's day* (March 1, the Welsh national holiday)

PISTOL
    Art thou his friend?
KING   And his kinsman too.
PISTOL
    The figo for thee then!   60
KING   I thank you. God be with you!
PISTOL
    My name is Pistol called.
KING   It sorts well with your fierceness.   63

                    Exit [Pistol]. [The] King [remains, aside].
            Enter Fluellen and Gower.
GOWER   Captain Fluellen!
FLUELLEN   So! in the name of Cheshu Christ, speak
    fewer. It is the greatest admiration in the universal orld, 66
    when the true and aunchient prerogatifes and laws of
    the wars is not kept. If you would take the pains but to
    examine the wars of Pompey the Great, you shall find, I   69
    warrant you, that there is not tiddle taddle nor pibble   70
    pabble in Pompey's camp. I warrant you, you shall find
    the ceremonies of the wars, and the cares of it, and the
    forms of it, and the sobriety of it, and the modesty of it,
    to be otherwise.
GOWER   Why, the enemy is loud; you hear him all
    night.
FLUELLEN   If the enemy is an ass and a fool and a prating   77
    coxcomb, is it meet, think you, that we should also,
    look you, be an ass and a fool and a prating coxcomb?
    In your own conscience now?   80
GOWER   I will speak lower.
FLUELLEN   I pray you and beseech you that you will.
                                    Exit [with Gower].

---

60 *figo* (cf. III.6.56)   **63** *sorts* suits   **66** *fewer* more quietly; *admiration* wonder   **69** *Pompey the Great* (Roman general defeated by Julius Caesar)   **70–
71** *pibble pabble* bibble babble, chatter   **77–78** *prating coxcomb* talkative
fool   **80** *In* on

KING
    Though it appear a little out of fashion,
    There is much care and valor in this Welshman.
      Enter three Soldiers, John Bates, Alexander Court, and
      Michael Williams.

COURT   Brother John Bates, is not that the morning which breaks yonder?

BATES   I think it be; but we have no great cause to desire the approach of day.

WILLIAMS   We see yonder the beginning of the day, but I
90 think we shall never see the end of it. Who goes there?

KING   A friend.

WILLIAMS   Under what captain serve you?

KING   Under Sir Thomas Erpingham.

WILLIAMS   A good old commander and a most kind gen-
95 tleman. I pray you, what thinks he of our estate?

96 KING   Even as men wracked upon a sand, that look to be washed off the next tide.

BATES   He hath not told his thought to the king?

99 KING   No; nor it is not meet he should. For though I
100 speak it to you, I think the king is but a man, as I am.
101 The violet smells to him as it doth to me; the element shows to him as it doth to me; all his senses have but
103 human conditions. His ceremonies laid by, in his nakedness he appears but a man; and though his
105 affections are higher mounted than ours, yet when they
106 stoop, they stoop with the like wing. Therefore, when
107 he sees reason of fears, as we do, his fears, out of doubt,
108 be of the same relish as ours are. Yet, in reason, no man
109 should possess him with any appearance of fear, lest he,
110 by showing it, should dishearten his army.

BATES   He may show what outward courage he will; but I believe, as cold a night as 'tis, he could wish himself in

---

95 *estate* condition 96 *wracked* shipwrecked 99 *meet* appropriate 101–2 *element shows* sky appears 103 *conditions* i.e., limitations; *ceremonies* observances due royalty 105 *affections* emotions 106 *stoop* swoop downward (hawking term); *with . . . wing* similarly 107 *of* for 108 *relish* taste 109 *possess him with* induce in him

Thames up to his neck; and so I would he were, and I   113
by him, at all adventures, so we were quit here.   114

KING   By my troth, I will speak my conscience of the
king: I think he would not wish himself anywhere but
where he is.

BATES   Then I would he were here alone. So should he be
sure to be ransomed, and a many poor men's lives
saved.   120

KING   I dare say you love him not so ill to wish him here
alone, howsoever you speak this to feel other men's   122
minds. Methinks I could not die anywhere so con-
tented as in the king's company, his cause being just
and his quarrel honorable.

WILLIAMS   That's more than we know.

BATES   Ay, or more than we should seek after, for we
know enough if we know we are the king's subjects. If
his cause be wrong, our obedience to the king wipes the
crime of it out of us.   130

WILLIAMS   But if the cause be not good, the king himself
hath a heavy reckoning to make when all those legs and   132
arms and heads, chopped off in a battle, shall join together at the latter day and cry all, "We died at such a   134
place," some swearing, some crying for a surgeon, some
upon their wives left poor behind them, some upon the
debts they owe, some upon their children rawly left. I   137
am afeared there are few die well that die in a battle; for
how can they charitably dispose of anything when   139
blood is their argument? Now, if these men do not die   140
well, it will be a black matter for the king that led them
to it; who to disobey were against all proportion of sub-   142
jection.

KING   So, if a son that is by his father sent about mer-
chandise do sinfully miscarry upon the sea, the

---

113 *Thames* (London's river, flowing past the Globe Theater)   114 *at all adventures* by all means; *quit* quit of, departed from   122 *feel* judge, detect
132 *reckoning* accounting   134 *latter day* i.e., the Christian Last Judgment
137 *rawly* unprepared   139 *charitably* in Christian love   142–43 *proportion
of subjection* due obedience

146   imputation of his wickedness, by your rule, should be
imposed upon his father that sent him; or if a servant,
under his master's command transporting a sum of
money, be assailed by robbers and die in many
150   irreconciled iniquities, you may call the business of the
master the author of the servant's damnation. But this
is not so. The king is not bound to answer the particular endings of his soldiers, the father of his son, nor the
154   master of his servant; for they purpose not their death
when they purpose their services. Besides, there is no
king, be his cause never so spotless, if it come to the
157   arbitrement of swords, can try it out with all unspotted
soldiers. Some peradventure have on them the guilt of
premeditated and contrived murder; some, of beguiling
160   virgins with the broken seals of perjury; some, making
161   the wars their bulwark, that have before gored the gentle bosom of peace with pillage and robbery. Now, if
163   these men have defeated the law and outrun native
punishment, though they can outstrip men, they have
165   no wings to fly from God. War is His beadle, war is His
vengeance; so that here men are punished for before-
breach of the king's laws in now the king's quarrel.
Where they feared the death, they have borne life away;
and where they would be safe, they perish. Then if they
170   die unprovided, no more is the king guilty of their
damnation than he was before guilty of those impieties
for the which they are now visited. Every subject's duty
is the king's, but every subject's soul is his own. Therefore should every soldier in the wars do as every sick
175   man in his bed – wash every mote out of his con-
176   science; and dying so, death is to him advantage; or not
dying, the time was blessedly lost wherein such prep-

---

146 *imputation of* blame for   150 *irreconciled* unabsolved   154 *purpose* intend   157 *arbitrement* judgment, decision making; *try* fight   161 *bulwark*
shield   163 *defeated* broken; *native* in their own country   165 *beadle* parish
officer who punishes petty crimes   170 *unprovided* spiritually unprepared
175 *mote* small impurity   176 *advantage* a gain (in that he dies prepared)

aration was gained; and in him that escapes, it were not
sin to think that, making God so free an offer, He let
him outlive that day to see His greatness and to teach   *180*
others how they should prepare.

WILLIAMS   'Tis certain, every man that dies ill, the ill
upon his own head – the king is not to answer it.

BATES   I do not desire he should answer for me, and yet I
determine to fight lustily for him.

KING   I myself heard the king say he would not be ransomed.

WILLIAMS   Ay, he said so, to make us fight cheerfully; but
when our throats are cut, he may be ransomed, and we
ne'er the wiser.   *190*

KING   If I live to see it, I will never trust his word after.

WILLIAMS   You pay him then! That's a perilous shot out
of an elder-gun that a poor and a private displeasure   *193*
can do against a monarch! You may as well go about to
turn the sun to ice with fanning in his face with a pea-
cock's feather. You'll never trust his word after! Come,
'tis a foolish saying.

KING   Your reproof is something too round. I should be   *198*
angry with you if the time were convenient.

WILLIAMS   Let it be a quarrel between us if you live.   *200*

KING   I embrace it.

WILLIAMS   How shall I know thee again?

KING   Give me any gage of thine, and I will wear it in my   *203*
bonnet. Then, if ever thou dar'st acknowledge it, I will   *204*
make it my quarrel.

WILLIAMS   Here's my glove. Give me another of thine.

KING   There.

WILLIAMS   This will I also wear in my cap. If ever thou
come to me and say, after tomorrow, "This is my
glove," by this hand, I will take thee a box on the ear.   *210*

KING   If ever I live to see it, I will challenge it.

---

193 *elder-gun* popgun   **198** *round* blunt   **203** *gage* token of challenge   **204**
bonnet headgear   **210** *take* give

WILLIAMS   Thou dar'st as well be hanged.

KING   Well, I will do it, though I take thee in the king's company.

WILLIAMS   Keep thy word. Fare thee well.

BATES   Be friends, you English fools, be friends! We have

217   French quarrels enow, if you could tell how to reckon.

218   KING   Indeed the French may lay twenty French crowns to one they will beat us, for they bear them on their

220   shoulders; but it is no English treason to cut French crowns, and tomorrow the king himself will be a clipper.   *Exit [Bates with other] Soldiers.*

Upon the king! Let us our lives, our souls,

224   Our debts, our careful wives,

Our children, and our sins, lay on the king!

We must bear all. O hard condition,

227   Twin-born with greatness, subject to the breath

Of every fool, whose sense no more can feel

229   But his own wringing! What infinite heart's ease

230   Must kings neglect that private men enjoy!

231   And what have kings that privates have not too,

232   Save ceremony, save general ceremony?

And what art thou, thou idol Ceremony?

What kind of god art thou, that suffer'st more

Of mortal griefs than do thy worshippers?

236   What are thy rents? what are thy comings-in?

O Ceremony, show me but thy worth!

238   What is thy soul of adoration?

Art thou aught else but place, degree, and form,

240   Creating awe and fear in other men?

Wherein thou art less happy being feared

---

217 *enow* enough; *reckon* count   218 *crowns* gold pieces (with play on "heads," since the English are outnumbered)   220 *cut* (1) clip, as in cutting the edges of (French) coins, a treasonable offense, (2) cut off, as in heads   224 *careful* careworn   227 *Twin-born with* inseparable from; *breath* gossip, opinion   229 *wringing* suffering   231 *privates* private citizens   232 *ceremony* royal pomp   236 *comings-in* revenues, returns   238 *soul of adoration* i.e., true essence of, or reason for, worship

Than they in fearing.
What drink'st thou oft, instead of homage sweet,
But poisoned flattery? O, be sick, great greatness,
And bid thy ceremony give thee cure!
Think'st thou the fiery fever will go out
With titles blown from adulation?   247
Will it give place to flexure and low bending?   248
Canst thou, when thou command'st the beggar's knee,
Command the health of it? No, thou proud dream,   250
That play'st so subtly with a king's repose.
I am a king that find thee; and I know   252
'Tis not the balm, the sceptre, and the ball,   253
The sword, the mace, the crown imperial,   254
The intertissued robe of gold and pearl,   255
The farcèd title running 'fore the king,   256
The throne he sits on, nor the tide of pomp
That beats upon the high shore of this world –
No, not all these, thrice-gorgeous ceremony,
Not all these, laid in bed majestical,   260
Can sleep so soundly as the wretched slave,
Who, with a body filled, and vacant mind,
Gets him to rest, crammed with distressful bread;   263
Never sees horrid night, the child of hell;
But like a lackey, from the rise to set,   265
Sweats in the eye of Phoebus, and all night   266
Sleeps in Elysium; next day after dawn,   267
Doth rise and help Hyperion to his horse;   268
And follows so the ever-running year
With profitable labor to his grave;   270
And but for ceremony, such a wretch,

---

247 *blown from adulation* spoken hyperbolically by flatterers   248 *flexure* bowing   252 *find thee* expose thee   253 *balm* consecrated oil used in coronation   254 *mace* ceremonial staff   255 *intertissued* interwoven   256 *farcèd title* pompous name   263 *distressful* i.e., hard-earned (?)   265 *lackey* constant attendant; *rise to set* sunrise to sunset   266 *Phoebus* sun god   267 *Elysium* resting place of the blessed in Greek myth   268 *Hyperion* charioteer of the sun

Winding up days with toil and nights with sleep,
273   Had the forehand and vantage of a king.
274   The slave, a member of the country's peace,
275   Enjoys it; but in gross brain little wots
276   What watch the king keeps to maintain the peace,
277   Whose hours the peasant best advantages.
    Enter Erpingham.

ERPINGHAM
278   My lord, your nobles, jealous of your absence,
    Seek through your camp to find you.

KING   Good old knight,
280   Collect them all together at my tent.
    I'll be before thee.

ERPINGHAM   I shall do't, my lord.   *Exit.*

KING
    O God of battles, steel my soldiers' hearts,
    Possess them not with fear! Take from them now
284   The sense of reckoning, if th' opposèd numbers
    Pluck their hearts from them. Not today, O Lord,
    O, not today, think not upon the fault
287   My father made in compassing the crown!
288   I Richard's body have interrèd new;
    And on it have bestowed more contrite tears
290   Than from it issued forcèd drops of blood.
    Five hundred poor I have in yearly pay,
    Who twice a day their withered hands hold up
    Toward heaven to pardon blood;
294   And I have built two chantries,
    Where the sad and solemn priests sing still
    For Richard's soul. More will I do:
    Though all that I can do is nothing worth,

---

273 *Had* would have; *forehand* upper hand   274 *member* sharer   275 *wots* knows   276 *watch* wakeful guard   277 *advantages* benefits   278 *jealous of* concerned about   284 *sense of reckoning* ability to count   287 *compassing* obtaining   288 *Richard's* i.e., Richard II, deposed and ordered slain by Henry IV; *new* anew   294 *chantries* i.e., chapels where Masses are celebrated for the souls of the dead

Since that my penitence comes after all,   298
Imploring pardon.
    Enter Gloucester.
GLOUCESTER
  My liege!   300
KING
  My brother Gloucester's voice. Ay.
  I know thy errand; I will go with thee.
  The day, my friends, and all things stay for me.
                               Exeunt.

*

∾ **IV.2** *Enter the Dauphin, Orleans, Rambures, and Beaumont.*

ORLEANS
  The sun doth gild our armor. Up my lords!
DAUPHIN   Monte, cheval! My horse, varlet lacquais! Ha!   2
ORLEANS   O brave spirit!
DAUPHIN   Via les eaux et terre!   4
ORLEANS   Rien puis les air et feu?   5
DAUPHIN   Cieux! cousin Orleans.   6
    Enter Constable.
  Now, my Lord Constable?
CONSTABLE
  Hark how our steeds for present service neigh!   8
DAUPHIN
  Mount them and make incision in their hides,

---

298 *Since that* i.e., as shown by the fact that
   IV.2 The French camp **s.d.** *Beaumont* (a "ghost" character, appearing only in this one stage direction)   **2** *Monte, cheval* soar, horse (cf. III.7.11–18); *varlet lacquais* rascal groom   **4** *Via . . . terre* away waters and earth (i.e., streams and solid ground)   **5** *Rien . . . feu?* not also air and fire? (Orleans jestingly takes the Dauphin's *"eaux"* and *"terre"* to refer to two of the four elements over which his horse will soar, and asks if it will not also soar above the realms of air and fire)   **6** *Cieux* the heavens (to which, in the old cosmology, the realm of fire extended; the Dauphin has converted the joke into serious hyperbole)   **8** *present* immediate

10 That their hot blood may spin in English eyes
11 And dout them with superfluous courage, ha!
RAMBURES
    What, will you have them weep our horses' blood?
    How shall we then behold their natural tears?
        Enter Messenger.
MESSENGER
14 The English are embattled, you French peers.
CONSTABLE
    To horse, you gallant princes! straight to horse!
    Do but behold yond poor starvèd band,
17 And your fair show shall suck away their souls,
18 Leaving them but the shales and husks of men.
    There is not work enough for all our hands,
20 Scarce blood enough in all their sickly veins
21 To give each naked curtle axe a stain
    That our French gallants shall today draw out
    And sheathe for lack of sport. Let us but blow on them,
    The vapor of our valor will o'erturn them.
25 'Tis positive 'gainst all exceptions, lords,
    That our superfluous lackeys and our peasants,
    Who in unnecessary action swarm
    About our squares of battle, were enow
29 To purge this field of such a hilding foe,
30 Though we upon this mountain's basis by
31 Took stand for idle speculation:
    But that our honors must not. What's to say?
    A very little little let us do,
    And all is done. Then let the trumpets sound
35 The tucket sonance and the note to mount;
36 For our approach shall so much dare the field
    That England shall couch down in fear and yield.

---

10 *spin* spurt, gush   11 *dout* extinguish; *superfluous courage* i.e., blood we
can spare   14 *embattled* ranged for battle   17 *fair show* grand appearance
18 *shales* shells   21 *curtle-axe* cutlass   25 *exceptions* objections   29 *hilding*
worthless   30 *mountain's basis by* i.e., nearby foothill   31 *speculation* view-
ing   35 *tucket sonance* trumpet call   36 *dare* daze

Enter Grandpré.

GRANDPRÉ

Why do you stay so long, my lords of France?
Yond island carrions, desperate of their bones,   39
Ill-favoredly become the morning field.   40
Their ragged curtains poorly are let loose,   41
And our air shakes them passing scornfully.
Big Mars seems bankrupt in their beggared host   43
And faintly through a rusty beaver peeps.   44
The horsemen sit like fixèd candlesticks
With torch-staves in their hand; and their poor jades   46
Lob down their heads, dropping the hides and hips,   47
The gum down roping from their pale-dead eyes,   48
And in their pale dull mouths the gimmaled bit   49
Lies foul with chawed grass, still and motionless;   50
And their executors, the knavish crows,   51
Fly o'er them all, impatient for their hour.
Description cannot suit itself in words
To demonstrate the life of such a battle   54
In life so lifeless as it shows itself.   55

CONSTABLE

They have said their prayers, and they stay for death.   56

DAUPHIN

Shall we go send them dinners and fresh suits
And give their fasting horses provender,   58
And after fight with them?

CONSTABLE

I stay but for my guard. On to the field!   60
I will the banner from a trumpet take   61
And use it for my haste. Come, come away!
The sun is high, and we outwear the day.   *Exeunt.*   63

*

39 *carrions* cadavers; *desperate* despairing   40 *Ill-favoredly become* do not
grace   41 *curtains* flags   43 *Mars* the god of war   44 *beaver* visor   46
torch-staves candles (here, lances)   47 *Lob* droop   48 *gum* watery rheum;
roping dripping ropelike   49 *gimmaled* jointed   51 *executors* disposers of the
remains   54 *battle* army   55 *In life* in actuality   56 *stay* wait   58 *provender*
feed   60 *guard* (including flag bearer)   61 *trumpet* trumpeter   63 *outwear*
waste

∾ **IV.3** *Enter Gloucester, Bedford, Exeter, Erpingham with all his Host, Salisbury, and Westmoreland.*

GLOUCESTER
Where is the king?

BEDFORD
2 The king himself is rode to view their battle.

WESTMORELAND
Of fighting men they have full three-score thousand.

EXETER
There's five to one; besides, they all are fresh.

SALISBURY
God's arm strike with us! 'Tis a fearful odds.
6 God be wi' you, princes all; I'll to my charge.
If we no more meet till we meet in heaven,
Then joyfully, my noble Lord of Bedford,
My dear Lord Gloucester, and my good Lord Exeter,
10 And my kind kinsman, warriors all, adieu!

BEDFORD Farewell, good Salisbury, and good luck go with thee!

EXETER
Farewell, kind lord: fight valiantly today;
14 And yet I do thee wrong to mind thee of it,
15 For thou art framed of the firm truth of valor.
                                   [Exit Salisbury.]

BEDFORD
He is as full of valor as of kindness,
Princely in both.
   Enter the King.

WESTMORELAND O that we now had here
But one ten thousand of those men in England
That do no work today!

KING   What's he that wishes so?
20 My cousin Westmoreland? No, my fair cousin.
21 If we are marked to die, we are enow

_____

IV.3 The English camp 2 *battle* army 6 *charge* post 14 *mind* remind 15 *framed* made 21–22 *enow To do* enough to cause

To do our country loss; and if to live,
The fewer men, the greater share of honor.
God's will! I pray thee wish not one man more.
By Jove, I am not covetous for gold,
Nor care I who doth feed upon my cost;   26
It yearns me not if men my garments wear;   27
Such outward things dwell not in my desires:
But if it be a sin to covet honor,
I am the most offending soul alive.   30
No, faith, my coz, wish not a man from England.   31
God's peace! I would not lose so great an honor
As one man more methinks would share from me   33
For the best hope I have. O, do not wish one more!
Rather proclaim it, Westmoreland, through my host,
That he which hath no stomach to this fight,   36
Let him depart; his passport shall be made,
And crowns for convoy put into his purse.   38
We would not die in that man's company
That fears his fellowship to die with us.   40
This day is called the Feast of Crispian.   41
He that outlives this day, and comes safe home,
Will stand a-tiptoe when this day is named
And rouse him at the name of Crispian.
He that shall see this day, and live old age,   45
Will yearly on the vigil feast his neighbors   46
And say, "Tomorrow is Saint Crispian."
Then will he strip his sleeve and show his scars,
[And say, "These wounds I had on Crispin's day."]
Old men forget; yet all shall be forgot,   50
But he'll remember, with advantages,   51
What feats he did that day. Then shall our names,

---

26 *upon . . . cost* at my expense   27 *yearns* grieves   31 *coz* cousin, kinsman
33 *share* take (as his portion)   36 *stomach to* appetite for (the stomach was
thought the seat of courage)   38 *convoy* transport   40 *fears . . . fellowship*
who is afraid to risk his life in my company   41 *Feast of Crispian* October 25
(the brothers Crispianus and Crispinus were martyred c. A.D. 287; they became the patron saints of shoemakers)   45 *live* live until   46 *vigil* eve of a
feast day   51 *advantages* i.e., embellishments

Familiar in his mouth as household words –
Harry the King, Bedford and Exeter,
Warwick and Talbot, Salisbury and Gloucester –
Be in their flowing cups freshly remembered.
This story shall the good man teach his son;
And Crispin Crispian shall ne'er go by,
From this day to the ending of the world,

60 But we in it shall be rememberèd –
We few, we happy few, we band of brothers;
For he today that sheds his blood with me

63 Shall be my brother. Be he ne'er so vile,

64 This day shall gentle his condition;
And gentlemen in England now abed
Shall think themselves accursed they were not here,
And hold their manhoods cheap whiles any speaks
That fought with us upon Saint Crispin's day.
    Enter Salisbury.

SALISBURY

69 My sovereign lord, bestow yourself with speed.

70 The French are bravely in their battles set

71 And will with all expedience charge on us.

KING

All things are ready, if our minds be so.

WESTMORELAND

Perish the man whose mind is backward now!

KING

Thou dost not wish more help from England, coz?

WESTMORELAND

God's will, my liege! would you and I alone,
Without more help, could fight this royal battle!

KING

Why, now thou hast unwished five thousand men!

78 Which likes me better than to wish us one.
You know your places. God be with you all!

---

63 *vile* lowborn **64** *gentle his condition* raise his rank; ennoble **69** *bestow yourself* take your position **70** *bravely . . . set* splendidly ranged to fight in their battalions **71** *expedience* speed **78** *likes* pleases

Tucket. Enter Montjoy.

MONTJOY

Once more I come to know of thee, King Harry,   80
If for thy ransom thou wilt now compound,   81
Before thy most assurèd overthrow;
For certainly thou art so near the gulf
Thou needs must be englutted. Besides, in mercy,   84
The Constable desires thee thou wilt mind   85
Thy followers of repentance, that their souls
May make a peaceful and a sweet retire   87
From all these fields, where (wretches!) their poor bodies
Must lie and fester.

KING   Who hath sent thee now?

MONTJOY

The Constable of France.   90

KING

I pray thee bear my former answer back:
Bid them achieve me, and then sell my bones.   92
Good God! why should they mock poor fellows thus?
The man that once did sell the lion's skin
While the beast lived, was killed with hunting him.
A many of our bodies shall no doubt   96
Find native graves; upon the which, I trust,   97
Shall witness live in brass of this day's work;
And those that leave their valiant bones in France,
Dying like men, though buried in your dunghills,   100
They shall be famed; for there the sun shall greet them
And draw their honors reeking up to heaven,   102
Leaving their earthly parts to choke your clime,
The smell whereof shall breed a plague in France.
Mark then abounding valor in our English,   105
That, being dead, like to the bullet's crasing,   106
Break out into a second course of mischief,

---

81 *compound* come to terms   84 *englutted* swallowed up   85 *mind* remind
87 *retire* retreat   92 *achieve* win, capture   96 *A many* many   97 *native* in
England   97–98 *upon . . . work* on which testimony of today's achievements
will be commemorated in brass tablets   102 *reeking* breathing   105 *Mark*
notice   106 *crasing* grazing, rebounding

108   Killing in relapse of mortality.
        Let me speak proudly. Tell the Constable
110   We are but warriors for the working day.
        Our gayness and our gilt are all besmirched
112   With rainy marching in the painful field.
113   There's not a piece of feather in our host –
114   Good argument, I hope, we will not fly –
115   And time hath worn us into slovenry.
116   But, by the mass, our hearts are in the trim;
        And my poor soldiers tell me, yet ere night
118   They'll be in fresher robes, or they will pluck
        The gay new coats o'er the French soldiers' heads
120   And turn them out of service. If they do this,
        As, if God please, they shall, my ransom then
122   Will soon be levied. Herald, save thou thy labor.
123   Come thou no more for ransom, gentle herald.
124   They shall have none, I swear, but these my joints;
        Which if they have as I will leave 'em them,
        Shall yield them little, tell the Constable.

MONTJOY
        I shall, King Harry. And so fare thee well.
        Thou never shalt hear herald any more.   *Exit.*

KING
        I fear thou wilt once more come again for a ransom.
        Enter York.

YORK
130   My lord, most humbly on my knee I beg
131   The leading of the vaward.

KING
        Take it, brave York. Now soldiers, march away;
        And how thou pleasest, God, dispose the day!   *Exeunt.*

---

108 *in . . . mortality* i.e., while in the process of decaying **110** *warriors . . . day* i.e., workaday or commonplace soldiers **112** *painful* arduous **113** *piece of feather* decorative plume **114** *fly* i.e., in retreat **115** *slovenry* battered appearance **116** *in the trim* well fashioned **118** *in fresher robes* i.e., new-garbed in heaven **120** *turn . . . service* i.e., dismiss them stripped of their livery **122** *levied* collected (from the French themselves) **123** *gentle* noble **124** *joints* bones, corpse **131** *vaward* vanguard

∗

∾ **IV.4** *Alarum. Excursions. Enter Pistol, French Soldier,*
Boy.

PISTOL   Yield, cur!

FRENCH SOLDIER   Je pense que vous estes le gentil-   2
homme de bon qualité.

PISTOL   Qualitie calmie custure me! Art thou a gentle-   4
man? What is thy name? Discuss.   5

FRENCH SOLDIER   O Seigneur Dieu!

PISTOL
O Signieur Dew should be a gentleman.
Perpend my words, O Signieur Dew, and mark.   8
O Signieur Dew, thou diest on point of fox,   9
Except, O signieur, thou do give to me   10
Egregious ransom.   11

FRENCH SOLDIER   O, prenez miséricorde! ayez pitié de   12
moi!

PISTOL
Moy shall not serve. I will have forty moys,
Or I will fetch thy rim out at thy throat   15
In drops of crimson blood.

FRENCH SOLDIER   Est-il impossible d'eschapper le force   17
de ton bras?

PISTOL   Brass, cur?
Thou damnèd and luxurious mountain goat,   20
Offer'st me brass?

FRENCH SOLDIER   O, pardonnez-moi!

IV.4 The battlefield of Agincourt   2–3 *Je . . . qualité* I think you are a gentleman of rank   4 *Qualitie . . . me* (gibberish, echoing *qualité* in l. 3, together with the refrain of a popular ballad, "Callen o custare me"; the refrain
itself derives from an Irish line, "*Cailin ó chois tSúire me*," meaning "I am a
girl from beside the Suir")   5 *Discuss* declare   8 *Perpend* consider   9 *fox*
sword   11 *Egregious* extraordinary   12–13 *O . . . moi* O, have mercy! take
pity on me   15 *rim* belly lining   17–18 *Est-il . . . bras* is it impossible to es-
cape the strength of your arm   20 *luxurious* lecherous

PISTOL
Say'st thou me so? Is that a ton of moys?
Come higher, boy; ask me this slave in French
What is his name.

26 BOY   Escoute. Comment estes-vous appelé?

27 FRENCH SOLDIER   Monsieur le Fer.

BOY   He says his name is Master Fer.

29 PISTOL   Master Fer? I'll fer him, and firk him, and ferret

30 him! Discuss the same in French unto him.

BOY   I do not know the French for "fer," and "ferret,"
and "firk."

PISTOL
Bid him prepare, for I will cut his throat.

34 FRENCH SOLDIER   Que dit-il, monsieur?

35 BOY   Il me commande de vous dire que vous faites vous

36 prest; car ce soldat ici est disposé tout asture de couper
vostre gorge.

PISTOL
38 Owy, cuppe le gorge, permafoy,
Peasant, unless thou give me crowns, brave crowns,
40 O'ermangled shalt thou be by this my sword.

FRENCH SOLDIER   O, je vous supplie, pour l'amour de
Dieu, me pardonner! Je suis le gentilhomme de bon
maison. Gardez ma vie, et je vous donnerai deux cents
escus.

PISTOL
What are his words?

BOY   He prays you to save his life. He is a gentleman of a
47 good house, and for his ransom he will give you two
hundred crowns.

PISTOL
Tell him my fury shall abate, and I the crowns will take.

---

26 *Escoute . . . appelé* listen, what is your name   27 *Fer* iron (French)   29
firk beat; *ferret* worry   34 *Que . . . monsieur* what does he say, sir   35–37
Il . . . gorge he bids me tell you to prepare, for this soldier is disposed to cut
your throat at once   36 *asture* i.e., "*à cette heure,*" at once   38 *Owy* yes (*oui*);
permafoy by my faith (French *par ma foi*)   47 *house* family

FRENCH SOLDIER   Petit monsieur, que dit-il?   50

BOY   Encore qu'il est contre son jurement de pardonner   51
aucun prisonnier; néantmoins, pour les escus que vous
l'avez promis, il est content de vous donner le liberté, le
franchisement.

FRENCH SOLDIER   Sur mes genoux je vous donne mille
remercîmens; et je m'estime heureux que j'ai tombé
entre les mains d'un chevalier, je pense, le plus brave,
vaillant, et très-distingué seigneur d'Angleterre.

PISTOL
Expound unto me, boy.

BOY   He gives you, upon his knees, a thousand thanks;   60
and he esteems himself happy that he hath fallen into
the hands of one, as he thinks, the most brave, valor-
ous, and thrice-worthy signieur of England.

PISTOL
As I suck blood, I will some mercy show!   64
Follow me.   *[Exit.]*

BOY   Suivez-vous le grand capitaine.*[Exit French Soldier.]*
I did never know so full a voice issue from so empty a
heart; but the saying is true, "The empty vessel makes
the greatest sound." Bardolph and Nym had ten times
more valor than this roaring devil i' th' old play that   70
every one may pare his nails with a wooden dagger; and
they are both hanged; and so would this be, if he durst
steal anything adventurously. I must stay with the lack-
eys with the luggage of our camp. The French might
have a good prey of us, if he knew of it; for there is   75
none to guard it but boys.   *Exit.*

*

---

50 *Petit . . . dit-il* small sir, what says he   51–54 *Encore . . . franchisement* although it is against his oath to pardon any prisoner, still for the crowns you
have promised he is willing to give you liberty, freedom   64 *suck blood* (cf.
II.3.53–54)   70 *roaring devil* i.e., the devil or Vice in the old morality plays,
sometimes subjected to the indignity of having his claws pared   75 *good prey*
easy target, easy pickings

∾ **IV.5** *Enter Constable, Orleans, Bourbon, Dauphin, and Rambures.*

1 CONSTABLE   O diable!
2 ORLEANS   O Seigneur! le jour est perdu, tout est perdu!
DAUPHIN
3   Mort de ma vie! all is confounded, all!
    Reproach and everlasting shame
    Sits mocking in our plumes.
        A short alarum.
6   O meschante fortune! Do not run away.
CONSTABLE
    Why, all our ranks are broke.
DAUPHIN
8   O perdurable shame! Let's stab ourselves.
    Be these the wretches that we played at dice for?
ORLEANS
10   Is this the king we sent to for his ransom?
BOURBON
    Shame, and eternal shame! nothing but shame!
    Let us die in honor. Once more back again!
    And he that will not follow Bourbon now,
    Let him go hence, and with his cap in hand
15   Like a base pander hold the chamber door
16   Whilst by a slave, no gentler than my dog,
    His fairest daughter is contaminated.
CONSTABLE
18   Disorder, that hath spoiled us, friend us now!
19   Let us on heaps go offer up our lives.
ORLEANS
20   We are enow yet living in the field

IV.5 1 *O diable* O devil   2 *O . . . perdu* O Lord! the day is lost, all is lost
3 *Mort . . . vie* death of my life; *confounded* ruined   6 *O . . . fortune* O mali-
cious Fortune   8 *perdurable* everlasting   15 *pander* a go-between in adulter-
ous liaisons, one who brings a man to a woman   16 *no gentler* of no higher
status   18 *friend* befriend   19 *on* in

To smother up the English in our throngs,
If any order might be thought upon.

BOURBON

The devil take order now! I'll to the throng.
Let life be short; else shame will be too long.   *Exeunt.*

*

❧ **IV.6** *Alarum. Enter the King and his train, [Exeter,
and others] with Prisoners.*

KING

Well have we done, thrice-valiant countrymen;
But all's not done, yet keep the French the field.

EXETER

The Duke of York commends him to your majesty.

KING

Lives he, good uncle? Thrice within this hour
I saw him down; thrice up again and fighting.
From helmet to the spur all blood he was.

EXETER

In which array, brave soldier, doth he lie,
Larding the plain; and by his bloody side,   8
Yoke-fellow to his honor-owing wounds,
The noble Earl of Suffolk also lies.   10
Suffolk first died; and York, all haggled over,   11
Comes to him, where in gore he lay insteepèd,
And takes him by the beard, kisses the gashes
That bloodily did yawn upon his face,   14
And cries aloud, "Tarry, my cousin Suffolk!
My soul shall thine keep company to heaven.
Tarry, sweet soul, for mine, then fly abreast;   17
As in this glorious and well-foughten field
We kept together in our chivalry!"
Upon these words I came and cheered him up.   20

IV.6 8 *Larding* fattening, fertilizing   11 *haggled* hacked   14 *yawn* gape   17
abreast together (with mine)

21 He smiled me in the face, raught me his hand,
And with a feeble grip, says, "Dear my lord,
Commend my service to my sovereign."
So did he turn, and over Suffolk's neck
He threw his wounded arm and kissed his lips;
26 And so, espoused to death, with blood he sealed
A testament of noble-ending love.
The pretty and sweet manner of it forced
29 Those waters from me which I would have stopped;
30 But I had not so much of man in me,
31 And all my mother came into mine eyes
And gave me up to tears.
KING   I blame you not;
33 For hearing this, I must perforce compound
34 With my full eyes, or they will issue too.   *Alarum.*
But hark! what new alarum is this same?
The French have reinforced their scattered men.
Then every soldier kill his prisoners!
Give the word through.   *Exit [with others].*

＊

✺ **IV.7** *Enter Fluellen and Gower.*

FLUELLEN   Kill the poys and the luggage? 'Tis expressly
against the law of arms. 'Tis as arrant a piece of knav-
ery, mark you now, as can be offert. In your conscience,
now, is it not?
GOWER   'Tis certain there's not a boy left alive; and the
cowardly rascals that ran from the battle ha' done this
slaughter. Besides, they have burned and carried away
all that was in the king's tent; wherefore the king most
worthily hath caused every soldier to cut his prisoner's
10   throat. O, 'tis a gallant king!

---

21 *raught* reached; *me* i.e., to me   26 *espoused* married   29 *Those waters* i.e.,
tears   31 *mother* i.e., womanly tenderness   33 *compound* come to terms
34 *issue* run (tears)
    IV.7 The battlefield of Agincourt

FLUELLEN   Ay, he was porn at Monmouth, Captain 11
   Gower. What call you the town's name where Alexander the Pig was born.
GOWER   Alexander the Great.
FLUELLEN   Why, I pray you, is not "pig" great? The pig,
   or the great, or the mighty, or the huge, or the magnanimous are all one reckonings, save the phrase is a little
   variations.   18
GOWER   I think Alexander the Great was born in Mace-
   don. His father was called Philip of Macedon, as I take 20
   it.
FLUELLEN   I think it is in Macedon where Alexander is
   porn. I tell you, captain, if you look in the maps of the
   orld, I warrant you sall find, in the comparisons between Macedon and Monmouth, that the situations,
   look you, is poth alike. There is a river in Macedon,
   and there is also moreover a river at Monmouth. It is
   called Wye at Monmouth; but it is out of my prains
   what is the name of the other river. But 'tis all one; 'tis
   alike as my fingers is to my fingers, and there is salmons 30
   in poth. If you mark Alexander's life well, Harry of
   Monmouth's life is come after it indifferent well; for 32
   there is figures in all things. Alexander, God knows and 33
   you know, in his rages, and his furies, and his wraths,
   and his cholers, and his moods, and his displeasures,
   and his indignations, and also being a little intoxicates
   in his prains, did, in his ales and his angers, look you,
   kill his best friend, Cleitus.   38
GOWER   Our king is not like him in that. He never killed
   any of his friends.   40
FLUELLEN   It is not well done, mark you now, to take the
   tales out of my mouth ere it is made and finished. I
   speak but in the figures and comparisons of it. As

---

11 *Monmouth* i.e., in Wales   18 *variations* i.e., altered   32 *is come after* i.e.,
resembles   33 *figures* comparisons   38 *Cleitus* (friend of Alexander, slain for
praising Philip)

Alexander killed his friend Cleitus, being in his ales and
his cups, so also Harry Monmouth, being in his right
wits and his good judgments, turned away the fat
47   knight with the great pelly doublet. He was full of jests,
48   and gipes, and knaveries, and mocks. I have forgot his
name.

50 GOWER   Sir John Falstaff.

FLUELLEN   That is he. I'll tell you there is good men porn
at Monmouth.

GOWER   Here comes his majesty.

Alarum. Enter King Harry and Bourbon, [Warwick,
Gloucester, Exeter, and Herald] with Prisoners.
Flourish.

KING

I was not angry since I came to France
55   Until this instant. Take a trumpet, herald;
56   Ride thou unto the horsemen on yond hill.
If they will fight with us, bid them come down
58   Or void the field. They do offend our sight.
If they'll do neither, we will come to them
60   And make them skirr away as swift as stones
61   Enforcèd from the old Assyrian slings.
Besides, we'll cut the throats of those we have;
And not a man of them that we shall take
Shall taste our mercy. Go and tell them so.

[Exeunt Herald and Gower.]

Enter Montjoy.

EXETER

Here comes the herald of the French, my liege.

GLOUCESTER

His eyes are humbler than they used to be.

KING

How now? What means this, herald? Know'st thou not

---

47 *great pelly* stuffed belly   48 *gipes* japes, jokes   55 *trumpet* trumpeter   56
yond yonder   58 *void* leave, depart from   60 *skirr* flee   61 *Enforcèd* driven

That I have fined these bones of mine for ransom?   68
Com'st thou again for ransom?
HERALD   No, great king.
I come to thee for charitable license   70
That we may wander o'er this bloody field
To book our dead, and then to bury them;   72
To sort our nobles from our common men.
For many of our princes – woe the while! –
Lie drowned and soaked in mercenary blood.   75
So do our vulgar drench their peasant limbs
In blood of princes, and the wounded steeds
Fret fetlock-deep in gore and with wild rage   78
Yerk out their armèd heels at their dead masters,   79
Killing them twice. O, give us leave, great king,   80
To view the field in safety and dispose
Of their dead bodies.
KING   I tell thee truly, herald,
I know not if the day be ours or no;
For yet a many of your horsemen peer   84
And gallop o'er the field.
HERALD   The day is yours.
KING
Praisèd be God and not our strength for it!
What is this castle called that stands hard by?
HERALD
They call it Agincourt.
KING
Then call we this the field of Agincourt,
Fought on the day of Crispin Crispianus.   90
FLUELLEN   Your grandfather of famous memory, an't
please your majesty, and your great-uncle Edward the
Plack Prince of Wales, as I have read in the chronicles,   93
fought a most prave pattle here in France.   94

---

68 *fined* pledged   72 *book* register   75 *mercenary blood* blood of hired soldiers   78 *fetlock* (the first joint above a horse's hoof)   79 *Yerk* lash   84 *peer*
appear   93 *chronicles* histories   94 *pattle* Battle of Crécy (see I.2.105–10)

KING   They did, Fluellen.

FLUELLEN   Your majesty says very true. If your majesties
is remembered of it, the Welshmen did good service in
a garden where leeks did grow, wearing leeks in their
Monmouth caps; which your majesty know to this
hour is an honorable padge of the service; and I do believe your majesty takes no scorn to wear the leek upon
Saint Tavy's day.

KING
I wear it for a memorable honor;
For I am Welsh, you know, good countryman.

FLUELLEN   All the water in Wye cannot wash your
majesty's Welsh plood out of your pody, I can tell you
that. God pless it and preserve it, as long as it pleases
his grace, and his majesty too!

KING   Thanks, good my countryman.

FLUELLEN   By Cheshu, I am your majesty's countryman,
I care not who know it! I will confess it to all the orld. I
need not to be ashamed of your majesty, praised be
God, so long as your majesty is an honest man.

KING
God keep me so! Our heralds go with him.
      Enter Williams.
Bring me just notice of the numbers dead
On both our parts.   *[Exeunt Heralds with Montjoy.]*
          Call yonder fellow hither.

EXETER   Soldier, you must come to the king.

KING   Soldier, why wear'st thou that glove in thy cap?

WILLIAMS   An't please your majesty, 'tis the gage of one
that I should fight withal, if he be alive.

KING   An Englishman?

WILLIAMS   An't please your majesty, a rascal that swag-
gered with me last night; who, if 'a live and ever dare to
challenge this glove, I have sworn to take him a box o'

---

99 *Monmouth caps* flat round caps   102 *Saint Tavy's day* Saint David's day,
the holy day of the patron saint of Wales   115 *just notice* exact record

th' ear; or if I can see my glove in his cap, which he
swore, as he was a soldier, he would wear if alive, I will
strike it out soundly.

KING   What think you, Captain Fluellen? Is it fit this soldier keep his oath?

FLUELLEN   He is a craven and a villain else, an't please   130
your majesty, in my conscience.

KING   It may be his enemy is a gentleman of great sort,
quite from the answer of his degree.   133

FLUELLEN   Though he be as good a gentleman as the
devil is, as Lucifer and Belzebub himself, it is necessary,
look your grace, that he keep his vow and his oath. If he
be perjured, see you now, his reputation is as arrant a
villain and a jack sauce as ever his plack shoe trod upon   138
God's ground and his earth, in my conscience, law!

KING   Then keep thy vow, sirrah, when thou meet'st the   *140*
fellow.

WILLIAMS   So I will, my liege, as I live.

KING   Who serv'st thou under?

WILLIAMS   Under Captain Gower, my liege.

FLUELLEN   Gower is a good captain and is good knowledge and literatured in the wars.   146

KING   Call him hither to me, soldier.

WILLIAMS   I will, my liege.   *Exit.*

KING   Here, Fluellen; wear thou this favor for me and
stick it in thy cap. When Alençon and myself were   *150*
down together, I plucked this glove from his helm. If   151
any man challenge this, he is a friend to Alençon and
an enemy to our person. If thou encounter any such,
apprehend him, an thou dost me love.   154

FLUELLEN   Your grace does me as great honors as can be
desired in the hearts of his subjects. I would fain see the   156

---

130 *craven* coward; *villain* lowborn serf (villein)   133 *from . . . degree* above
responding to a challenge from one of his rank   138 *jack sauce* impudent
rascal; *as ever* as sure as   146 *literatured* well-read, learned   151 *helm* helmet
154 *an* if   156 *fain* eagerly

man, that has but two legs, that shall find himself
158 aggriefed at this glove, that is all. But I would fain see it
once, an please God of his grace that I might see.
160 KING   Know'st thou Gower?
FLUELLEN   He is my dear friend, an please you.
KING   Pray thee go seek him and bring him to my tent.
FLUELLEN   I will fetch him.   *Exit.*
KING
My Lord of Warwick, and my brother Gloucester,
Follow Fluellen closely at the heels.
166 The glove which I have given him for a favor
167 May haply purchase him a box o' th' ear;
It is the soldier's. I by bargain should
Wear it myself. Follow, good cousin Warwick.
170 If that the soldier strike him – as I judge
By his blunt bearing, he will keep his word –
Some sudden mischief may arise of it;
For I do know Fluellen valiant,
174 And, touched with choler, hot as gunpowder,
And quickly will return an injury.
Follow, and see there be no harm between them.
Go you with me, uncle of Exeter.   *Exeunt.*

*

∾ **IV.8** *Enter Gower and Williams.*

WILLIAMS   I warrant it is to knight you, captain.
       Enter Fluellen.
FLUELLEN   God's will and his pleasure, captain, I beseech
you now, come apace to the king. There is more good
4 toward you peradventure than is in your knowledge to
dream of.

---

158 *aggriefed* aggrieved, incensed   166 *favor* token   167 *haply* by chance
174 *touched . . . choler* i.e., quick-tempered
IV.8 The English camp   4 *peradventure* by chance

WILLIAMS   Sir, know you this glove?

FLUELLEN   Know the glove? I know the glove is a glove.

WILLIAMS   I know this; and thus I challenge it.
    Strikes him.

FLUELLEN   'Sblood! an arrant traitor as any's in the uni- 9
versal orld, or in France, or in England!   10

GOWER   How now, sir? You villain!

WILLIAMS   Do you think I'll be forsworn?   12

FLUELLEN   Stand away, Captain Gower. I will give treason his payment into plows, I warrant you.   14

WILLIAMS   I am no traitor.

FLUELLEN   That's a lie in thy throat. I charge you in his 16
majesty's name apprehend him. He's a friend of the
Duke Alençon's.
    Enter Warwick and Gloucester.

WARWICK   How now, how now? What's the matter?

FLUELLEN   My Lord of Warwick, here is, praised be God 20
for it, a most contagious treason come to light, look 21
you, as you shall desire in a summer's day. Here is his
majesty.
    Enter King and Exeter.

KING   How now? What's the matter?

FLUELLEN   My liege, here is a villain and a traitor that,
look your grace, has struck the glove which your
majesty is take out of the helmet of Alençon.

WILLIAMS   My liege, this was my glove, here is the fellow 28
of it; and he that I gave it to in change promised to 29
wear it in his cap. I promised to strike him if he did. I 30
met this man with my glove in his cap, and I have been
as good as my word.

FLUELLEN   Your majesty hear now, saving your majesty's
manhood, what an arrant, rascally, peggarly, lousy
knave it is! I hope your majesty is pear me testimony

---

9 *'Sblood* (by) Christ's blood   12 *forsworn* brought to break an oath   14 *his*
its   16 *lie . . . throat* unforgivable falsehood   21 *contagious* noxious   28 *fellow* mate   29 *change* exchange

36   and witness, and will avouchment, that this is the glove
of Alençon that your majesty is give me, in your conscience, now.

KING

Give me thy glove, soldier. Look, here is the fellow of it.
40   'Twas I indeed thou promisèd'st to strike;
And thou hast given me most bitter terms.

42   FLUELLEN An please your majesty, let his neck answer
for it, if there is any martial law in the orld.

KING How canst thou make me satisfaction?

WILLIAMS All offenses, my lord, come from the heart.
Never came any from mine that might offend your
majesty.

KING It was ourself thou didst abuse.

WILLIAMS Your majesty came not like yourself. You ap-
50   peared to me but as a common man; witness the night,
51   your garments, your lowliness. And what your highness
suffered under that shape, I beseech you take it for your
own fault, and not mine; for had you been as I took
you for, I made no offense. Therefore I beseech your
highness pardon me.

KING

Here, uncle Exeter, fill this glove with crowns
And give it to this fellow. Keep it, fellow,
And wear it for an honor in thy cap
Till I do challenge it. Give him the crowns;
60   And captain, you must needs be friends with him.

FLUELLEN By this day and this light, the fellow has
62   mettle enough in his pelly. Hold, there is twelve pence
for you; and I pray you to serve God, and keep you out
of prawls, and prabbles, and quarrels, and dissensions,
and, I warrant you, it is the petter for you.

WILLIAMS I will none of your money.

FLUELLEN It is with a good will. I can tell you it will
serve you to mend your shoes. Come, wherefore should

---

36 *avouchment* i.e., avouch   42 *An* if   51 *lowliness* i.e., humble bearing   62
mettle i.e., courage

you be so pashful? Your shoes is not so good. 'Tis a
good silling, I warrant you, or I will change it.   70
Enter [an English] Herald.

KING

Now, herald, are the dead numb'red?

HERALD

Here is the number of the slaught'red French.
[Gives a paper.]

KING

What prisoners of good sort are taken, uncle?   73

EXETER

Charles Duke of Orleans, nephew to the king;
John Duke of Bourbon and Lord Bouciqualt:
Of other lords and barons, knights and squires,
Full fifteen hundred, besides common men.

KING

This note doth tell me of ten thousand French
That in the field lie slain. Of princes, in this number,
And nobles bearing banners, there lie dead   80
One hundred twenty-six; added to these,
Of knights, esquires, and gallant gentlemen,
Eight thousand and four hundred; of the which,
Five hundred were but yesterday dubbed knights;   84
So that in these ten thousand they have lost   85
There are but sixteen hundred mercenaries;
The rest are princes, barons, lords, knights, squires,
And gentlemen of blood and quality.
The names of those their nobles that lie dead:
Charles Delabreth, High Constable of France;   90
Jacques of Chatillon, Admiral of France;
The master of the crossbows, Lord Rambures;
Great Master of France, the brave Sir Guichard
    Dauphin;

---

70 *silling* shilling (a coin)   73 *good sort* high rank   80 *bearing banners* with
coats of arms (cf. IV.2.61–62)   84 *dubbed* made, named   85 *ten thousand*
(the mortality figures are from Hall and Holinshed; the modern estimate is
about 7,000)

John Duke of Alençon; Anthony Duke of Brabant,
The brother to the Duke of Burgundy;
And Edward Duke of Bar; of lusty earls,
Grandpré and Roussi, Faulconbridge and Foix,
Beaumont and Marle, Vaudemont and Lestrale.
Here was a royal fellowship of death!
100   Where is the number of our English dead?
    [Herald gives another paper.]
    Edward the Duke of York, the earl of Suffolk,
102   Sir Richard Ketly, Davy Gam, esquire;
103   None else of name; and of all other men
104   But five-and-twenty. O God, thy arm was here!
    And not to us, but to thy arm alone,
106   Ascribe we all! When, without stratagem,
    But in plain shock and even play of battle,
    Was ever known so great and little loss
109   On one part and on th' other? Take it, God,
110   For it is none but thine!
EXETER   'Tis wonderful!
KING
    Come, go we in procession to the village;
    And be it death proclaimèd through our host
    To boast of this, or take that praise from God
    Which is His only.
FLUELLEN   Is it not lawful, an please your majesty, to tell
    how many is killed?
KING
    Yes, captain; but with this acknowledgment,
    That God fought for us.
FLUELLEN   Yes, my conscience, He did us great good.
KING
120   Do we all holy rites.

---

102 *Davy Gam* David ap Llewellyn   103 *name* high birth   104 *five-and-twenty* (the figure given by Hall; the modern estimate is about 450)   106 *Ascribe* attribute, credit; *stratagem* policy, craft   109 *Take it* i.e., take the credit

Let there be sung "Non nobis" and "Te Deum,"   121
The dead with charity enclosed in clay,
And then to Calais; and to England then;
Where ne'er from France arrived more happy men.   124

          Exeunt.

*

∾ **V.Cho.** *Enter Chorus.*

Vouchsafe to those that have not read the story   1
That I may prompt them; and of such as have,
I humbly pray them to admit th' excuse   3
Of time, of numbers, and due course of things
Which cannot in their huge and proper life
Be here presented. Now we bear the king
Toward Calais. Grant him there. There seen,
Heave him away upon your wingèd thoughts
Athwart the sea. Behold, the English beach   9
Pales in the flood with men, wives, and boys,   10
Whose shouts and claps outvoice the deep-mouthed sea,
Which, like a mighty whiffler 'fore the king,   12
Seems to prepare his way. So let him land,
And solemnly see him set on to London.
So swift a pace hath thought that even now
You may imagine him upon Blackheath;   16
Where that his lords desire him to have borne   17
His bruisèd helmet and his bended sword
Before him through the city. He forbids it,
Being free from vainness and self-glorious pride;   20

---

121 *Non nobis* i.e., Psalm 115, beginning in English "Not unto us, O Lord, not unto us, but unto thy name give glory"; *Te Deum* song of thanksgiving, beginning in English "We praise thee, O God"   124 *happy* fortunate
 V.Cho.   1 *Vouchsafe* permit, allow   3 *admit th' excuse* i.e., tolerate the treatment   9 *Athwart* across   10 *Pales* hems; *flood* sea   12 *whiffler* attendant clearing the way for a procession   16 *Blackheath* (area southeast of London)   17 *Where that* where

21   Giving full trophy, signal, and ostent
       Quite from himself to God. But now behold,
23   In the quick forge and working-house of thought,
       How London doth pour out her citizens!
25   The mayor and all his brethren in best sort,
       Like to the senators of th' antique Rome,
       With the plebeians swarming at their heels,
       Go forth and fetch their conquering Caesar in;
29   As, by a lower but by loving likelihood,
30   Were now the general of our gracious empress,
       As in good time he may, from Ireland coming,
32   Bringing rebellion broachèd on his sword,
       How many would the peaceful city quit
       To welcome him! Much more, and much more cause,
       Did they this Harry. Now in London place him;
36   As yet the lamentation of the French
       Invites the King of England's stay at home;
38   The emperor's coming in behalf of France
       To order peace between them; and omit
40   All the occurrences, whatever chanced,
       Till Harry's back-return again to France.
42   There must we bring him; and myself have played
43   The interim, by remembering you 'tis past.
44   Then brook abridgment; and your eyes advance,
       After your thoughts, straight back again to France.

                                    Exit.

*

---

21 *signal, and ostent* token and show (of victory) 23 *quick . . . thought* i.e., nimble, creative imagination 25 *sort* array 29 *lower . . . likelihood* less exalted but devoted comparison 30 *general* i.e., Robert Devereux, Earl of Essex, whose abortive Irish campaign ended in September 1599; *empress* i.e., Elizabeth I 32 *broachèd* impaled 36 *As . . . lamentation* while the continuing state of dejection 38 *emperor's coming* i.e., the Holy Roman Emperor Sigismund's mission to England in May 1416 42–43 *played The interim* filled up the interval 43 *remembering* reminding 44 *brook* tolerate

⤳ **V.1** *Enter Fluellen and Gower.*

GOWER   Nay, that's right. But why wear you your leek today? Saint Davy's day is past.

FLUELLEN   There is occasions and causes why and wherefore in all things. I will tell you ass my friend, Captain Gower. The rascally, scald, peggarly, lousy, pragging 5 knave, Pistol, which you and yourself and all the orld know to be no petter than a fellow, look you now, of no 7 merits, he is come to me and prings me pread and salt yesterday, look you, and pid me eat my leek. It was in a place where I could not preed no contention with him; 10 but I will be so pold as to wear it in my cap till I see him once again, and then I will tell him a little piece of my desires.

     Enter Pistol.

GOWER   Why, here he comes, swelling like a turkey cock.

FLUELLEN   'Tis no matter for his swellings nor his turkey cocks. God pless you, Aunchient Pistol! you scurvy, lousy knave, God pless you!

PISTOL

Ha! art thou bedlam? Dost thou thirst, base Trojan,   18
To have me fold up Parca's fatal web?   19
Hence! I am qualmish at the smell of leek.   20

FLUELLEN   I peseech you heartily, scurvy, lousy knave, at 21 my desires, and my requests, and my petitions, to eat, look you, this leek. Because, look you, you do not love it, nor your affections and your appetites and your disgestions does not agree with it, I would desire you to eat it.

PISTOL

Not for Cadwallader and all his goats.   26

FLUELLEN   There is one goat for you. *(Strikes him.)* Will you be so good, scald knave, as eat it?

V.1 The English camp   **5** *scald* scurvy   **7** *fellow* i.e., groom   **10** *preed* i.e., breed, foment   **18** *bedlam* crazy; *Trojan* rascal   **19** *fold . . . web* i.e., complete the design of the Parcae (Fates) by ending your life   **20** *qualmish* nauseous   **21** *peseech* i.e., beseech   **26** *Cadwallader* (last of the Welsh, or British, kings); *goats* (associated with Welsh poverty)

PISTOL
>Base Trojan, thou shalt die!

30 FLUELLEN   You say very true, scald knave, when God's
>will is. I will desire you to live in the meantime, and eat
>your victuals. Come, there is sauce for it. *[Strikes him.]*
33   You called me yesterday mountain-squire; but I will
34   make you today a squire of low degree. I pray you fall
>to. If you can mock a leek, you can eat a leek.

36 GOWER   Enough, captain. You have astonished him.

FLUELLEN   I say I will make him eat some part of my
38   leek, or I will peat his pate four days. – Pite, I pray you.
39   It is good for your green wound and your ploody cox-
40   comb.

PISTOL   Must I bite?

FLUELLEN   Yes, certainly, and out of doubt, and out of
>question too, and ambiguities.

PISTOL   By this leek, I will most horribly revenge. I eat
>and eat, I swear.

FLUELLEN   Eat, I pray you. Will you have some more
>sauce to your leek? There is not enough leek to swear
>by.

PISTOL   Quiet thy cudgel, thou dost see I eat.

50 FLUELLEN   Much good do you, scald knave, heartily.
>Nay, pray you throw none away, the skin is good for
>your proken coxcomb. When you take occasions to see
>leeks hereafter, I pray you mock at 'em; that is all.

PISTOL   Good.

55 FLUELLEN   Ay, leeks is good. Hold you, there is a groat to
>heal your pate.

PISTOL   Me a groat?

FLUELLEN   Yes verily, and in truth you shall take it, or I
>have another leek in my pocket which you shall eat.

---

33 *mountain-squire* i.e., lord over mountainous land, and hence unprofitable
(for anything but grazing goats)   34–35 *fall to* begin eating   36 *astonished*
dazed   38 *pate* head   39 *green* raw;   39–40 *coxcomb* fool's scalp   55 *groat*
fourpenny piece

PISTOL

 I take thy groat in earnest of revenge.   60

FLUELLEN If I owe you anything, I will pay you in
 cudgels. You shall be a woodmonger and buy nothing
 of me but cudgels. God be wi' you, and keep you, and
 heal your pate.   *Exit.*

PISTOL

 All hell shall stir for this!

GOWER Go, go. You are a counterfeit cowardly knave.
 Will you mock at an ancient tradition, begun upon an
 honorable respect and won as a memorable trophy of   68
 predeceased valor, and dare not avouch in your deeds
 any of your words? I have seen you gleeking and galling   70
 at this gentleman twice or thrice. You thought, because
 he could not speak English in the native garb, he could
 not therefore handle an English cudgel. You find it otherwise, and henceforth let a Welsh correction teach you
 a good English condition. Fare ye well.   *Exit.*

PISTOL

 Doth Fortune play the huswife with me now?   76
 News have I, that my Doll is dead i' th' spital   77
 Of a malady of France;   78
 And there my rendezvous is quite cut off.   79
 Old I do wax, and from my weary limbs   80
 Honor is cudgeled. Well, bawd I'll turn,
 And something lean to cutpurse of quick hand.   82
 To England will I steal, and there I'll steal;
 And patches will I get unto these cudgeled scars
 And swear I got them in the Gallia wars.   *Exit.*   85

*

---

60 *in earnest of* as a down payment for **68** *respect* consideration **70** *gleek-*
ing and galling gibing and scoffing **76** *huswife* hussy, unfaithful woman
77 *Doll* (error for Nell); *spital* hospital **78** *malady of France* i.e., venereal
disease **79** *rendezvous* meeting, refuge **80** *wax* grow **82** *something . . .*
hand i.e., lean to quick-handed purse-cutting **85** *Gallia* French

∾ **V.2** *Enter, at one door, King Henry, Exeter, Bedford,*
[Gloucester,] Warwick, [Westmoreland,] and other
Lords; at another, Queen Isabel, the [French] King, the
Duke of Burgundy, [the Princess Katherine, Alice,]
and other French.

KING HENRY
    Peace to this meeting, wherefore we are met.
2   Unto our brother France and to our sister
    Health and fair time of day. Joy and good wishes
    To our most fair and princely cousin Katherine.
5   And as a branch and member of this royalty,
6   By whom this great assembly is contrived,
    We do salute you, Duke of Burgundy.
    And, princes French, and peers, health to you all.

FRANCE
    Right joyous are we to behold your face,
10   Most worthy brother England. Fairly met.
    So are you, princes English, every one.

QUEEN
12   So happy be the issue, brother England,
    Of this good day and of this gracious meeting
    As we are now glad to behold your eyes –
    Your eyes which hitherto have borne in them,
16   Against the French that met them in their bent,
17   The fatal balls of murdering basilisks.
    The venom of such looks, we fairly hope,
    Have lost their quality, and that this day
20   Shall change all griefs and quarrels into love.

KING HENRY
    To cry amen to that, thus we appear.

QUEEN
    You English princes all, I do salute you.

V.2 Within the palace of the French king at Troyes **2** *our sister* i.e., Queen
of France **5** *royalty* royal family **6** *contrived* arranged **12** *issue* outcome,
result **16** *in their bent* in the direction of their glance **17** *basilisks* monsters
that killed with a look – here, cannons

BURGUNDY

My duty to you both, on equal love,
Great Kings of France and England! That I have labored
With all my wits, my pains, and strong endeavors
To bring your most imperial majesties
Unto this bar and royal interview,   27
Your mightiness on both parts best can witness.
Since, then, my office hath so far prevailed
That, face to face and royal eye to eye,   *30*
You have congreeted, let it not disgrace me   31
If I demand before this royal view,
What rub or what impediment there is
Why that the naked, poor, and mangled peace,
Dear nurse of arts, plenties, and joyful births,
Should not, in this best garden of the world,
Our fertile France, put up her lovely visage.   37
Alas, she hath from France too long been chased,
And all her husbandry doth lie on heaps,   39
Corrupting in it own fertility.   40
Her vine, the merry cheerer of the heart,
Unprunèd dies; her hedges even-pleached,   42
Like prisoners wildly overgrown with hair,
Put forth disordered twigs; her fallow leas   44
The darnel, hemlock, and rank fumitory   45
Doth root upon, while that the coulter rusts   46
That should deracinate such savagery.   47
The even mead, that erst brought sweetly forth   48
The freckled cowslip, burnet, and green clover,   49
Wanting the scythe, all uncorrected, rank,   50
Conceives by idleness, and nothing teems   51
But hateful docks, rough thistles, kecksies, burrs,   52
Losing both beauty and utility.

---

27 *bar* court of justice   31 *congreeted* greeted each other; *disgrace* ill become
37 *put up* show   39 *husbandry* agricultural produce, harvest   40 *it* its   42
even-pleached evenly intertwined   44 *fallow leas* untilled open fields   45
darnel . . . fumitory i.e., weeds   46 *coulter* plow blade   47 *deracinate* uproot
48 *even mead* smooth meadow; *erst* formerly   49 *cowslip, burnet* herbs   50
Wanting lacking   51 *Conceives* breeds (weeds)   52 *kecksies* kexes, dry stems

And all our vineyards, fallows, meads, and hedges,
55   Defective in their natures, grow to wildness.
56   Even so our houses and ourselves and children
Have lost, or do not learn for want of time,
58   The sciences that should become our country;
But grow like savages, as soldiers will,
60   That nothing do but meditate on blood,
61   To swearing and stern looks, diffused attire,
And everything that seems unnatural.
63   Which to reduce into our former favor
64   You are assembled; and my speech entreats
65   That I may know the let why gentle peace
Should not expel these inconveniences
And bless us with her former qualities.

KING HENRY
68   If, Duke of Burgundy, you would the peace
69   Whose want gives growth to th' imperfections
70   Which you have cited, you must buy that peace
71   With full accord to all our just demands;
72   Whose tenors and particular effects
73   You have, enscheduled briefly, in your hands.

BURGUNDY
The king hath heard them; to the which as yet
There is no answer made.

KING HENRY   Well then, the peace,
Which you before so urged, lies in his answer.

FRANCE
77   I have but with a cursitory eye
78   O'erglanced the articles. Pleaseth your grace
To appoint some of your council presently
80   To sit with us once more, with better heed

---

55 *Defective* i.e., fallen, blighted by original sin   56 *houses* households   58
sciences knowledge, skills   61 *diffused* disordered   63 *reduce* restore; *favor*
appearance   64 *entreats* begs   65 *let* hindrance   68 *would* wish   69 *want*
lack, absence   71 *accord* assent   72 *tenors* gist   73 *enscheduled* listed   77
cursitory cursory   78 *Pleaseth* may it please   80 *heed* attention

To resurvey them, we will suddenly   81
Pass our accept and peremptory answer.   82

KING HENRY
Brother, we shall. Go, uncle Exeter,
And brother Clarence, and you, brother Gloucester,
Warwick, and Huntingdon, go with the king;
And take with you free power to ratify,
Augment, or alter, as your wisdoms best
Shall see advantageable for our dignity,   88
Anything in or out of our demands,
And we'll consign thereto. Will you, fair sister,   90
Go with the princes or stay here with us?

QUEEN
Our gracious brother, I will go with them.
Happily a woman's voice may do some good   93
When articles too nicely urged be stood on.   94

KING HENRY
Yet leave our cousin Katherine here with us.
She is our capital demand, comprised   96
Within the forerank of our articles.   97

QUEEN
She hath good leave.
          Exeunt [all but] King [Henry] and Katherine [and
          Alice].

KING HENRY   Fair Katherine, and most fair,
Will you vouchsafe to teach a soldier terms
Such as will enter at a lady's ear   *100*
And plead his love suit to her gentle heart?   101

KATHERINE   Your majesty shall mock at me. I cannot
speak your England.

KING HENRY   O fair Katherine, if you will love me
soundly with your French heart, I will be glad to hear
you confess it brokenly with your English tongue. Do
you like me, Kate?

---

81 *suddenly* swiftly   82 *Pass* deliver   88 *advantageable* advantageous to   90
consign consent   93 *Happily* haply, perchance   94 *nicely* punctiliously   96
capital chief   97 *forerank* forefront, first row   101 *suit* cause

KATHERINE   Pardonnez-moi, I cannot tell wat is "like me."

110 KING HENRY   An angel is like you, Kate, and you are like an angel.

112 KATHERINE   Que dit-il? Que je suis semblable à les anges?

114 ALICE   Oui, vraiment, sauf vostre grace, ainsi dit-il.

KING HENRY   I said so, dear Katherine, and I must not blush to affirm it.

KATHERINE   O bon Dieu! les langues des hommes sont pleine de tromperies.

KING HENRY   What says she, fair one? that the tongues of
120 men are full of deceits?

ALICE   Oui, dat de tongues of de mans is be full of deceits. Dat is de princesse.

123 KING HENRY   The princess is the better Englishwoman. I' faith, Kate, my wooing is fit for thy understanding. I am glad thou canst speak no better English; for if thou couldst, thou wouldst find me such a plain king that thou wouldst think I had sold my farm to buy my
128 crown. I know no ways to mince it in love but directly to say, "I love you." Then, if you urge me farther than
130 to say, "Do you in faith?" I wear out my suit. Give me
131 your answer, i' faith, do: and so clap hands and a bargain. How say you, lady?

133 KATHERINE   Sauf vostre honneur, me understand well.

134 KING HENRY   Marry, if you would put me to verses or to dance for your sake, Kate, why, you undid me. For the
136 one I have neither words nor measure; and for the
137 other I have no strength in measure, yet a reasonable measure in strength. If I could win a lady at leapfrog, or

---

112–13 *Que . . . anges?* what does he say? That I am like the angels?   114 *Oui . . . dit-il* yes, truly, save your grace, so he says   123 *better Englishwoman* (because disdainful of flattery)   128 *mince it* speak flirtatiously   130 *wear . . . suit* exhaust my terms of courtship   131 *clap* shake   133 *Sauf vostre honneur* saving your honor   134 *put . . . verses* ask me to recite/write poetry   136 *measure* metier   137 *in measure* at dancing by vaulting into my saddle with my armor on my back, under the correction of bragging be it spoken, I should 140 quickly leap into a wife. Or if I might buffet for my 141 love, or bound my horse for her favors, I could lay on 142 like a butcher and sit like a jackanapes, never off. But, 143 before God, Kate, I cannot look greenly, not gasp out 144 my eloquence, nor I have no cunning in protestation, 145 only downright oaths which I never use till urged, nor even break for urging. If thou canst love a fellow of this temper, Kate, whose face is not worth sunburning, that 148 never looks in his glass for love of anything he sees 149 there, let thine eye be thy cook. I speak to thee plain 150 soldier. If thou canst love me for this, take me; if not, to say to thee that I shall die, is true; but for thy love, by 152 the Lord, no; yet I love thee too. And while thou liv'st, dear Kate, take a fellow of plain and uncoined con- 154 stancy, for he perforce must do thee right, because he hath not the gift to woo in other places. For these fellows of infinite tongue that can rhyme themselves into ladies' favors, they do always reason themselves out again. What! A speaker is but a prater; a rhyme is but a ballad. A good leg will fall, a straight back will stoop, 160 a black beard will turn white, a curled pate will grow bald, a fair face will wither, a full eye will wax hollow; but a good heart, Kate, is the sun and the moon; or rather, the sun, and not the moon, for it shines bright and never changes, but keeps his course truly. If thou would have such a one, take me; and take me, take a soldier; take a soldier, take a king. And what say'st thou then to my love? Speak, my fair, and fairly, I pray thee.

---

140 *under . . . spoken* though to say so may be reproved as bragging   141 *buffet* fight, box   142 *bound* make prance; *lay on* go to it   143 *like a butcher* i.e., bloodily; *jackanapes* monkey   144 *greenly* wanly   145 *protestation* i.e., swearing love   148 *temper* character, temperament   149 *glass* mirror   150 *cook* preparer of food   150–51 *plain soldier* in the blunt manner of a fighting man   152 *die* (with pun on orgasm)   154 *uncoined* not prepared for circulation   160 *fall* diminish

KATHERINE   Is it possible dat I sould love de *ennemie* of France?

KING HENRY   No, it is not possible you should love the enemy of France, Kate; but in loving me you should love the friend of France, for I love France so well that I will not part with a village of it – I will have it all mine. And, Kate, when France is mine and I am yours, then yours is France and you are mine.

KATHERINE   I cannot tell wat is dat.

KING HENRY   No, Kate? I will tell thee in French, which I am sure will hang upon my tongue like a new-married wife about her husband's neck, hardly to be shook off. Je quand sur le possession de France, et quand vous avez le possession de moi (let me see, what then? Saint Denis be my speed!), donc vostre est France et vous estes mienne. It is as easy for me, Kate, to conquer the kingdom as to speak so much more French. I shall never move thee in French, unless it be to laugh at me.

KATHERINE   Sauf vostre honneur, le François que vous parlez, il est meilleur que l'Anglois lequel je parle.

KING HENRY   No, faith, is't not, Kate. But thy speaking of my tongue, and I thine, most truly-falsely, must needs be granted to be much at one. But, Kate, dost thou understand thus much English? Canst thou love me?

KATHERINE   I cannot tell.

KING HENRY   Can any of your neighbors tell, Kate? I'll ask them. Come, I know thou lovest me; and at night when you come into your closet, you'll question this gentlewoman about me, and I know, Kate, you will to her dispraise those parts in me that you love with your heart; but, good Kate, mock me mercifully, the rather,

---

181–82 *Je quand . . . moi* (Henry's bad attempt to paraphrase ll. 175–76) 182–83 *Saint Denis* (patron saint of France)   183 *be my speed* give me help, luck   187–88 *Sauf . . . parle* save your honor, the French you speak is better than the English I speak   197 *closet* private room

gentle princess, because I love thee cruelly. If ever thou
beest mine, Kate, as I have a saving faith within me tells
me thou shalt, I get thee with scambling, and thou   203
must therefore needs prove a good soldier-breeder.
Shall not thou and I, between Saint Denis and Saint
George, compound a boy, half French, half English,
that shall go to Constantinople and take the Turk by   207
the beard? Shall we not? What say'st thou, my fair
flower-de-luce?   209

KATHERINE   I do not know dat.   210

KING HENRY   No; 'tis hereafter to know, but now to
promise. Do but now promise, Kate, you will endeavor
for your French part of such a boy, and for my English
moiety take the word of a king and a bachelor. How an-   214
swer you, la plus belle Katherine du monde, mon   215
trèscher et devin déesse?

KATHERINE   Your majestee ave fausse French enough to   217
deceive de most sage demoiselle dat is en France.   218

KING HENRY   Now, fie upon my false French! By mine
honor in true English, I love thee, Kate; by which   220
honor I dare not swear thou lovest me; yet my blood
begins to flatter me that thou dost, notwithstanding
the poor and untempering effect of my visage. Now   223
beshrew my father's ambition! He was thinking of civil   224
wars when he got me; therefore was I created with a   225
stubborn outside, with an aspect of iron, that when I   226
come to woo ladies, I fright them. But in faith, Kate,
the elder I wax the better I shall appear. My comfort is
that old age, that ill layer-up of beauty, can do no more   229
spoil upon my face. Thou hast me, if thou hast me, at   230
the worst; and thou shalt wear me, if thou wear me,

---

203 *scambling* scrambling for possessions, snatching   207 *Turk* i.e., the infi-
del   209 *flower-de-luce* fleur-de-lis (the emblem of France)   214 *moiety* half
215–16 *la . . . déesse* the most beautiful Katherine of the world, my very dear
and divine goddess   217 *fausse* false   218 *sage* wise; *demoiselle* young lady
223 *untempering* unpropitiating; *visage* face   224 *beshrew* curse   225 *got me*
conceived me   226 *aspect* appearance   229 *ill layer-up* poor provider of

better and better; and therefore tell me, most fair
Katherine, will you have me? Put off your maiden
234   blushes; avouch the thoughts of your heart with the
looks of an empress; take me by the hand, and say,
"Harry of England, I am thine!" which word thou shalt
no sooner bless mine ear withal but I will tell thee
aloud, "England is thine, Ireland is thine, France is
thine, and Henry Plantagenet is thine"; who, though I
240   speak it before his face, if he be not fellow with the best
king, thou shalt find the best king of good fellows.
Come, your answer in broken music! for thy voice is
music and thy English broken; therefore, queen of all,
244   Katherine, break thy mind to me in broken English.
Wilt thou have me?

246 KATHERINE   Dat is as it sall please de roi mon père.

KING HENRY   Nay, it will please him well, Kate; it shall
please him, Kate.

KATHERINE   Den it sall also content me.

250 KING HENRY   Upon that I kiss your hand and I call you
my queen.

252 KATHERINE   Laissez, mon seigneur, laissez, laissez! Ma
foi, je ne veux point que vous abaissiez vostre grandeur
en baisant le main d'une de vostre seigneurie indigne
serviteur. Excusez-moi, je vous supplie, mon très-
puissant seigneur.

KING HENRY   Then I will kiss your lips, Kate.

KATHERINE   Les dames et demoiselles pour estre baisée
devant leur nopces, il n'est pas la coutume de France.

260 KING HENRY   Madam my interpreter, what says she?

ALICE   Dat it is not be de fashon pour le ladies of
France – I cannot tell wat is "baiser" en Anglish.

KING HENRY   To kiss.

---

234 *avouch* confirm, guarantee   240 *fellow with* equal to   244 *break thy
mind* reveal your decision   246 *de . . . père* the king my father   252–56
Laissez . . . seigneur desist, my lord, desist, desist! My faith, I do not wish you
to lower your dignity by kissing the hand of your lordship's unworthy servant. Excuse me, I pray you, my all-powerful lord

ALICE   Your majestee entendre bettre que moi.   264

KING HENRY   It is not a fashion for the maids in France
to kiss before they are married, would she say?

ALICE   Oui, vraiment.   267

KING HENRY   O Kate, nice customs curtsy to great kings.   268
Dear Kate, you and I cannot be confined within the
weak list of a country's fashion. We are the makers of   270
manners, Kate; and the liberty that follows our places   271
stops the mouth of all findfaults, as I will do yours for
upholding the nice fashion of your country in denying   273
me a kiss. Therefore patiently, and yielding. *[Kisses her.]*
You have witchcraft in your lips, Kate. There is more
eloquence in a sugar touch of them than in the tongues
of the French Council, and they should sooner per-
suade Harry of England than a general petition of
monarchs. Here comes your father.

Enter the French Power and the English Lords.

BURGUNDY   God save your majesty! My royal cousin,   280
teach you our princess English?

KING HENRY   I would have her learn, my fair cousin, how
perfectly I love her, and that is good English.

BURGUNDY   Is she not apt?

KING HENRY   Our tongue is rough, coz, and my
condition is not smooth; so that, having neither the   286
voice nor the heart of flattery about me, I cannot so
conjure up the spirit of love in her that he will appear
in his true likeness.   289

BURGUNDY   Pardon the frankness of my mirth if I an-   290
swer you for that. If you would conjure in her, you
must make a circle; if conjure up love in her in his true
likeness, he must appear naked and blind. Can you   293
blame her then, being a maid yet rosed over with the   294

---

264 *entendre* understands 267 *Oui, vraiment* yes, truly 268 *nice* strict,
(over-) precise 270 *list* border 271 *follows our places* attends our rank
273 *nice* fastidious 286 *condition* personality 289 *likeness* image 293
naked and blind i.e., like Cupid 294 *yet rosed over* still blushing

virgin crimson of modesty, if she deny the appearance
of a naked blind boy in her naked seeing self? It were,
297   my lord, a hard condition for a maid to consign to.

298   KING HENRY   Yet they do wink and yield, as love is blind
and enforces.

300   BURGUNDY   They are then excused, my lord, when they
see not what they do.

KING HENRY   Then, good my lord, teach your cousin to
consent winking.

BURGUNDY   I will wink on her to consent, my lord, if
you will teach her to know my meaning; for maids
306   well summered and warm kept are like flies at
307   Bartholomew-tide, blind, though they have their eyes;
and then they will endure handling which before
would not abide looking on.

310   KING HENRY   This moral ties me over to time and a hot
summer; and so I shall catch the fly, your cousin, in the
latter end, and she must be blind too.

BURGUNDY   As love is, my lord, before it loves.

KING HENRY   It is so; and you may, some of you, thank
315   love for my blindness, who cannot see many a fair
French city for one fair French maid that stands in my
way.

318   FRANCE   Yes, my lord, you see them perspectively, the
cities turned into a maid; for they are all girdled with
320   maiden walls that war hath never entered.

KING HENRY   Shall Kate be my wife?

FRANCE   So please you.

---

297 *hard condition* (1) difficult situation, (2) male erection; *consign* consent
298 *wink* shut eyes   **306** *well summered* i.e., carefully nurtured   **306–7**
like . . . Bartholomew-tide i.e., sluggish in the heat of summer   **307**
(Bartholomew-tide is August 24)   **315–17** *who . . . way* (Henry forgoes possession of certain territories in exchange for Katherine's hand in marriage)
318 *perspectively* i.e., through an optic glass (which multiplies images)   **320**
maiden virginal

KING HENRY   I am content, so the maiden cities you talk
  of may wait on her. So the maid that stood in the way   324
  for my wish shall show me the way to my will.

FRANCE
  We have consented to all terms of reason.

KING HENRY
  Is't so, my lords of England?

WESTMORELAND
  The king hath granted every article:
  His daughter first; and in sequel all,
  According to their firm proposèd natures.   330

EXETER   Only   he   hath   not   yet   subscribèd   this: 331
  Where your majesty demands that the King of France,
  having any occasion to write for matter of grant, shall   333
  name   your   highness   in   this   form   and   with   this
  addition, in French, "Nostre très-cher fils Henri, Roi   335
  d'Angleterre, Héritier de France"; and thus in Latin,
  "Praeclarissimus filius noster Henricus, Rex Angliae et
  Haeres Franciae."

FRANCE
  Nor this I have not, brother, so denied
  But your request shall make me let it pass.   340

KING HENRY
  I pray you then, in love and dear alliance,
  Let that one article rank with the rest,
  And thereupon give me your daughter.

FRANCE
  Take her, fair son, and from her blood raise up
  Issue to me, that the contending kingdoms
  Of France and England, whose very shores look pale   346
  With envy of each other's happiness,
  May cease their hatred, and this dear conjunction
  Plant neighborhood and Christian-like accord

---

324 *wait on her* serve as her entourage (i.e., dowry)   330 *firm . . . natures*
strict stipulations   331 *subscribèd* agreed to   333 *for . . . grant* in official
deeds granting lands   335 *addition* title   335–38 *Nostre . . . France; . . .
Praeclarissimus . . . Franciae* our dear son Henry, King of England and heir of
France   346 *look pale* i.e., with their chalk cliffs

350 In their sweet bosoms, that never war advance
His bleeding sword 'twixt England and fair France.

LORDS   Amen!

KING HENRY
Now, welcome, Kate; and bear me witness all
That here I kiss her as my sovereign queen.
Flourish.

QUEEN
God, the best maker of all marriages,
Combine your hearts in one, your realms in one!
As man and wife, being two, are one in love,
So be there 'twixt your kingdoms such a spousal
359 That never may ill office, or fell jealousy,
360 Which troubles oft the bed of blessèd marriage,
361 Thrust in between the paction of these kingdoms
To make divorce of their incorporate league;
That English may as French, French Englishmen,
Receive each other! God speak this Amen!

ALL   Amen!

KING HENRY
Prepare we for our marriage; on which day,
My Lord of Burgundy, we'll take your oath,
368 And all the peers', for surety of our leagues.
Then shall I swear to Kate, and you to me,
370 And may our oaths well kept and prosperous be!
Sennet. Exeunt.

*

∾ **Epilogue** *Enter Chorus.*

Thus far, with rough and all-unable pen,
2   Our bending author hath pursued the story,
In little room confining mighty men,

---

359 *ill office* evil dealing; *fell* cruel   361 *paction* pact   368 *surety . . . leagues* guarantee of our alliances
    Epi.   2 *bending* (1) bowing, (2) manipulating (of historical material)

Mangling by starts the full course of their glory.   4
Small time; but in that small most greatly lived   5
  This Star of England. Fortune made his sword,
By which the world's best garden he achieved,   7
  And of it left his son imperial lord.
Henry the Sixth, in infant bands crowned king   9
  Of France and England, did this king succeed;   10
Whose state so many had the managing
  That they lost France and made his England bleed:
Which oft our stage hath shown; and for their sake,   13
In your fair minds let this acceptance take.   14

---

4 *Mangling by starts* misrepresenting in fragments   5 *Small time* (Henry V's reign was brief: he died in 1422 aged 35, after 9 years' rule)   7 *best garden* i.e., France (cf. V.2.36)   9 *infant bands* swaddling clothes   13 *hath shown* i.e., in Shakespeare's *Henry VI* plays; *for their sake* i.e., inasmuch as they have pleased you   14 *this* this play

NOW AVAILABLE

Antony and Cleopatra
ISBN 0-14-071452-9

The Comedy of Errors
ISBN 0-14-071474-X

Coriolanus
ISBN 0-14-071473-1

Cymbeline
ISBN 0-14-071472-3

Henry IV, Part I
ISBN 0-14-071456-1

Henry IV, Part 2
ISBN 0-14-071457-X

Henry V
ISBN 0-14-071458-8

King Lear
ISBN 0-14-071476-6

King Lear (The Quarto and Folio Texts)
ISBN 0-14-071490-1

Macbeth
ISBN 0-14-071478-2

Much Ado About Nothing
ISBN 0-14-071480-4

The Narrative Poems
ISBN 0-14-071481-2

Richard III
ISBN 0-14-071483-9

Romeo and Juliet
ISBN 0-14-071484-7

The Tempest
ISBN 0-14-071485-5

Timon of Athens
ISBN 0-14-071487-1

Titus Andronicus
ISBN 0-14-071491-X

Twelfth Night
ISBN 0-14-071489-8

The Two Gentlemen of Verona
ISBN 0-14-071461-8

The Winter's Tale
ISBN 0-14-071488-X

FORTHCOMING

All's Well That Ends Well
ISBN 0-14-071460-X

As You Like It
ISBN 0-14-071471-5

Hamlet
ISBN 0-14-071454-5

Henry VI, Part 1
ISBN 0-14-071465-0

Henry VI, Part 2
ISBN 0-14-071466-9

Henry VI, Part 3
ISBN 0-14-071467-7

Henry VIII
ISBN 0-14-071475-8

Julius Caesar
ISBN 0-14-071468-5

King John
ISBN 0-14-071459-6

Love's Labor's Lost
ISBN 0-14-071477-4

Measure for Measure
ISBN 0-14-071479-0

The Merchant of Venice
ISBN 0-14-071462-6

The Merry Wives of Windsor
ISBN 0-14-071464-2

A Midsummer Night's Dream
ISBN 0-14-071455-3

Othello
ISBN 0-14-071463-4

Pericles
ISBN 0-14-071469-3

Richard II
ISBN 0-14-071482-0

The Sonnets
ISBN 0-14-071453-7

The Taming of the Shrew
ISBN 0-14-071451-0

Troilus and Cressida
ISBN 0-14-071486-3